MULTILINGUAL ASPECTS
OF INFORMATION
TECHNOLOGY

Multilingual Aspects of Information Technology

P. A. Bennett
R. L. Johnson
J. McNaught
J. M. Pugh
J. C. Sager
H. L. Somers

Centre for Computational
Linguistics,
University of Manchester
Institute of Science
and Technology

Gower

Published by
Gower Publishing Company Limited
Gower House
Croft Road
Aldershot
Hants GU11 3HR
England

Gower Publishing Company
Old Post Road
Brookfield
Vermont 05036
USA

British Library Cataloguing in Publication Data

Multilingual aspects of information
  technology.
  1. Linguistics——Data processing
  I. Bennett, P. A.
  410'.28'5   P98

ISBN 0 566 03513 8

Printed and bound in Great Britain by
Biddles Ltd, Guildford and King's Lynn

Contents

Preface

This book is an introduction to the multilingual aspects of what has become known as Information Technology (IT) – the use of computers to process, store and disseminate information. In a multilingual world, IT quickly comes up against the 'language barrier'. At the same time, however, computers contribute to overcoming this barrier, through the use of dictionaries, thesauri, translation systems and information retrieval systems on machine. Up till now, however, there have been no works which give an overview of this whole field, and this is what we have set out to provide. Generally, we have presented the current state of the field; where we have put forward views on controversial issues or on future trends of development, we have made it clear that these are our own views.

This work is aimed at readers of various types. For students of modern languages and linguistics, it is a guide to areas which should be increasingly claiming their attention, while computer science students will find that it opens their eyes to new applications of their skills. For professional language teachers, translators and lexicographers who are interested in the impact of computers on their work, it will be a handy introduction and work of reference. Researchers in linguistics, computational linguistics and artificial intelligence will be able to use it as a reference for an aspect of these disciplines which receives too little attention other than from a few specialist workers. Finally, the general reader interested in the impact of computers on society will find up-to-date information on such topics as 'can computers translate?'.

We have relied greatly on our experience of teaching the BSc. course in Computational Linguistics and Modern Languages at UMIST. However, aiming the book at readers of a variety of backgrounds has presented a number of problems for us. Chapter 1 sketches some of the relevant aspects of the contributing disciplines, and provides a certain amount of background knowledge. Most of the book, however, can be understood without any specialised knowledge. We have deliberately provided numerous references to other works, both introductory and advanced, to enable readers to acquire any necessary background for themselves, and to follow up any areas of particular interest. We hope that the book will provide readers with sufficient understanding to pursue further work in any of the areas covered.

In order not to disfigure the text with references, we have relegated sources of information and suggestions for further reading to sections at the end of each chapter. As far as possible, we have referred only to works in English. In the interests of recommending works easily available to both student and general reader, we have pursued a deliberate policy of referring primarily to books, secondarily to articles in journals and conference proceedings, and only when essential to unpublished works such as technical reports.

We should like to express our appreciation to all our colleagues in the Centre for Computational Linguistics at UMIST for providing the stimulating environment which enabled us to produce this book.

Lexical innovation is subject to certain principles which permit the creation of completely new forms and meanings (the process of neology), the creation of new forms for existing meanings (resulting in synonymy), the application of new meanings to existing forms (i.e. transfer of meaning resulting in homonymy) and the combination of existing words and word elements into new lexemes (through the processes of composition and derivation). Lexeme formation rules are quite different from those governing sentence formation. They are typically selective in their application and therefore of more limited range, and the norms which restrict their applicability are much more arbitrary and hence less predictable than those governing grammar. For example, the prefix un- is currently accepted in <u>unintelligent</u> but not in *unclever (the asterisk is used before ill-formed expressions), and the suffix -ment may be attached to the verb <u>govern</u> but not to rule. Finally, and most significantly for lexicography, the applicability of lexeme formation rules changes much more quickly than that of grammatical rules. New words and meanings enter a language at a much faster rate than syntactic changes. An accompanying feature of the speed of lexical change is that new words are open to attract additional meanings by emotive association or connotation which they did not have at their inception – consider for example the term <u>artificial intelligence</u>.

The size and dynamism of the lexicon creates huge problems for its collection and representation; conventional printed dictionaries have proved to be a particularly inadequate means of representing lexical data. Production processes are notoriously slow, making it impossible for printed dictionaries to keep pace with lexical change so that they are out-of-date by the time they are published. They are also incomplete because their limited size compels the lexicographer to be selective in the choice of entries and in the amount of information that is to be associated with any one item. The alphabetic ordering of entries, which is the organisational hallmark of most printed dictionaries, obfuscates grammatical and semantic relations between lexemes and serves merely to underline the arbitrariness of association of written form with meaning. Finally, their layout, which is dictated by commercial constraints, is inflexible and heavily redundant and makes the process of dictionary consultation complex and unwieldy.

Today dictionaries are used in greater numbers than ever before, though their importance as reference tools which assist in communication and learning dates back thousands of years. Yet, despite considerable developments in linguistic and lexicological research (see 1.2), the nature of dictionaries has not altered significantly. Until quite recently, methods of data collection, modes of dictionary compilation, and the presentation of the final product had remained essentially unchanged. The main trend which has characterised the development of lexicography is that towards increased specialisation and diversification of dictionary types. Nevertheless, the general, multifunctional dictionary has continued to dominate the market.

With the growth of international communication the importance of interlingual (bi- and multilingual) dictionaries has soared. In fact, dictionaries for translation are historically prior to monolingual dictionaries and evidence suggests they originated as early as 3000 BC. Multilingual lexicography faces all the problems described above with the additional difficulty of establishing, within a closed static medium, valid correspondences between the elements of two or more open, dynamic systems which may exhibit different cultural and linguistic behaviour and even divergent concept structures.

Lexicographers have long been aware of the drawbacks of their traditional working methods, the inevitable subjectivity of which has provoked accusations of lack of scientific rigour. The application of information technology has revolutionised lexicography, opening up a whole new range of possibilities and has overcome many of its previous shortcomings. The introduction of data base techniques and the use of large machine-readable corpora of texts have facilitated radical improvements so that new forms of dictionaries, new methods of compilation, and new modes of use of dictionaries now exist. In specialised (i.e. terminological) lexicography, the benefits of automation have led to the proliferation of terminological data banks which have become an established tool for the dissemination of accurate, up-to-date terms in several languages. An overview of the progress in these areas is given in Chapters 2 and 3.

1.4 COMPUTER SCIENCE

The development of computers has provided the technology which makes possible the existence of this book's topic, so we shall introduce computer science, though without going into any detail about program writing or the electronic make-up of computers.

A computer is an electronic machine which takes various data as input, processes them in some way and produces output in the form of information. Its distinguishing features are speed and accuracy, very large storage capacity and versatility. The physical units comprising a computer system - the hardware - include a central processor (which performs the basic operations), various kinds of storage devices or memory (which store data) and input and output devices such as keyboards, printers and visual display units. Software is the set of instructions - or programs - which control the operation of the hardware. These programs are written in programming languages, which enable the programmer to write instructions clearly and concisely without worrying about the low-level detail of how the computer implements the instructions. A program written in such a 'high-level' language is also relatively easy to transfer from one computer to another. As an example, consider the following statement from the language Pascal:

$$X := Y + 1$$

This is an instruction to give X the value of Y plus 1, and replaces a long sequence of instructions at 'machine code' level. Relieved of concern about such matters as in which location of the memory the value of Y is stored (which is likely to vary each time the program is run), the programmer is free to concentrate on the overall design and structure of the program. A language such as Pascal encourages the programmer to structure the program in terms of the logical sub-parts of the problem being tackled. A complex program typically consists of procedures, each of which performs some specific sub-task and is called into action at an appropriate point; the building blocks of a program are simple statements such as the one above.

At an abstract level, then, a computer may be seen as a device for manipulating data. Commonly, these data take the form of numbers, with the computer being used as a kind of giant calculating machine. But from the early days of high-level languages, there have been programs designed to handle non-numeric data. A high-level language usually needs a compiler, a program which accepts the text of a program written in one programming language and outputs an equivalent program in another, lower-level language. The structure of a number of programming languages (including Algol 60 and Pascal) is described by the formalism known as BNF (Backus-Naur Form or Backus Normal Form), which is very similar to that for phrase-structure rules used in linguistics (see 1.2). The BNF grammar can be used to find the structure of a syntactically correct program; by associating procedures with the grammar rules, the translation of each piece of program structure into the desired lower-level form can be done as the structure is recognised.

Given such 'syntax-directed compilation', it is a short step to see that computers can be used to manipulate texts in natural, and not just programming, languages. The relative simplicity, and total lack of ambiguity, of programming languages means that the construction of a compiler presents different problems from that of a program to analyse natural language, but the point is that non-numeric (or symbolic) computation is in no way alien to the foundations of computer science.

Currently, the commonest language used for natural language processing is Lisp. Lisp (for LISt Processing), one of the oldest high-level languages, is particularly fitted for symbolic computation because of its suitability for handling lists and other appropriate data structures, and because (unlike Algol and Pascal) it is a functional rather than a procedural language. This means that a program consists not of instructions to the computer to perform some action but of expressions to be evaluated. If the Lisp expression (plus 3 5) is input to a computer, 8 will be returned as the result of the evaluation (e.g. shown on the screen of a visual display unit).

The information which a computer outputs may take the form of, for example, an updated bank balance or a projection of a nation's future economic development. The term 'information technology' (IT) is becoming increasingly fashionable to describe the use of computers to store, process and disseminate information. The practical applications examined in 1.6 below may be regarded as parts of IT.

Another term which should be mentioned is 'artificial intelligence' (AI), the branch of computer science devoted to enabling computers to employ knowledge and draw inferences in such a way as to appear to be behaving intelligently. Expert systems, for example, can be regarded as applications of AI techniques. Exactly what counts as AI is controversial, and perhaps mainly terminological; in particular, the content of this present book should not be construed as implying that all the topics dealt with are really instances of AI.

1.5 COMPUTATIONAL LINGUISTICS

Computational linguistics (CL) is the result of the marriage of linguistics and computer science. As such, it is concerned with the processing of natural language: this rubric covers the understanding and synthesis of speech, and the analysis and generation of written texts. If a text in natural language is input to the computer, the output can take any of several forms, depending on the nature of the program: the aim may be recognition (deciding whether a string of words forms a grammatical sentence), parsing (assigning a syntactic structure to a sentence) or translation (in which we include translation both into some semantic or logical representation, and also into another natural language).

Let us concentrate on parsing, and adopt a slightly simplified version of the phrase-structure rules given earlier in 1.2, i.e.

(2a) S ---> NP VP
(2b) NP ---> DET N

A parsing program, or parser, could exploit rule (2b) as follows: if a string contains a determiner followed by a noun, it will create a noun phrase node which dominates just these two elements. This illustrates a 'bottom-up' approach to parsing: a phrase-marker (see 1.2) is built from the bottom upwards, by combining together increasingly higher-level constituents. For instance, after a noun phrase and a verb phrase have been constructed, these can be combined together by consulting rule (2a) to build a node dominating an entire sentence.

An alternative approach is 'top-down' parsing: the parser begins by 'attempting' to build a sentence constituent. Rule (2a) shows that to build a sentence, it is necessary first to construct a noun phrase followed by a verb phrase, and rule (2b) states that a noun phrase can consist of a determiner followed by a noun. The parser then examines the first word in the string: if this is a determiner, the parser goes on to examine the next word. If this is a noun, the parser has completed the processing of a noun phrase, and can go on to try to build a verb phrase.

We now turn to a problem which arises when there is more than one rule which a parser may apply at some point in the parsing of a string. Suppose a top-down parser, parsing The cat ate the mouse, is attempting to construct a verb phrase, and that the grammar it applies has these two rules:

(3a) VP ---> V PP
(3b) VP ---> V NP

There are two possible strategies which may be employed in such situations. One is known as parallel processing: all the possibilities are taken 'at once', i.e. the parser not only attempts to build a verb phrase consisting of verb plus prepositional phrase, but also one consisting of verb plus noun phrase. So after the verb has been processed, the parser will attempt to build both a noun phrase and a verb phrase, by consulting the appropriate grammatical rules. In our example, only a noun phrase will be built, and so only rule (3b) will enable the construction of a verb phrase.

The alternative to parallel processing is backtracking. Only one of the possibilities is tried initially, and if this results in failure, the parser backtracks to the point where the 'wrong' path was followed. In our example, suppose the parser first tries to apply (3a). It will be unable to match the mouse to a prepositional phrase, and so will have to go back and 'try again' using (3b), which will succeed. Both parallel-processing and backtracking strategies, then, may involve the partial building of structure which is then 'thrown away' in that it plays no part in the phrase-marker assigned to a sentence.

For certain classes of grammar, both top-down and bottom-up approaches can use the same grammar, the difference being in how the grammatical rules are interpreted. So there is a separation of the declarative statement of the structure of the language (cf. the native speaker's linguistic competence) and the strategies used to interpret this information. The same grammar can be used by parsing algorithms (an algorithm is a set of instructions which is guaranteed to produce a definite result within a finite period of time) which employ quite different strategies; conversely, a single algorithm can be used with different grammars (even grammars of different languages). Ideally, either grammar or parsing algorithm can be modified without affecting the other.

The experience of constructing compilers for programming languages (see 1.4) means that there is a great deal known about parsing with context-free grammars (grammars which only use rules like those in (2a) and (2b)). A number of tried and tested parsing algorithms are known which work quickly and efficiently. The celebrated Earley algorithm for context-free grammars is guaranteed to parse a sentence in a time proportional to the cube of its length, at most. However, since elegance of description is also a crucial consideration, parsing criteria cannot in themselves determine the optimal choice of a grammar for natural language.

Parsing a sentence in order to build a syntactic representation for it is only rarely an end in itself. The syntactic structure will usually serve as input to some further processing, typically semantically-oriented. For instance, in a question-answering system, the aim will be to translate the sentence into a representation in some formal query language, this representation being the basis of the interrogation of some data base of knowledge (whether of airline flights or the contents of the British Library catalogue, to name but two of a myriad of possible applications). The next section develops these matters further.

1.6 CURRENT AREAS OF APPLICATION

In order to aid the reader in appreciating the diversity of current applications of CL, and how these relate to each other, we choose to give a general classification of systems. Right at the outset, we note that this classification is somewhat idealised, as many systems can in fact be multiply classified. However we refrain from this here, preferring to refer only to major characteristics or objectives of particular systems.

1.6.1 Systems which take a text or message and transform it somehow

The obvious example here is that of a machine translation (MT) system, which transforms a text expressed in one language to an equivalent text expressed in another (or several other) language(s). This transformation does not usually affect the overall length, contents or form of the text, but it can be said to cause variations along the multilingual dimension. The principles of MT are discussed in Chapter 4.

Less obviously, perhaps, there are systems which attempt to generate reduced, monolingual forms of texts, i.e. abstracts or extracts. Abstracting, whether manual or automatic, is an important activity in today's technological society, where access to primary sources is becoming increasingly difficult due to the exponential growth in the volume of information available. Readers today have no time to keep abreast of developments even in a small specialised field. The problem is compounded by the existence of language barriers. An interim answer is provided by abstracting services, which provide abstracts of current literature, hence saving perusal of whole documents, and by on-line bibliographic data bases, which will return bibliographical references in response to a search expressed in combinations of keywords with which documents are indexed. Often, such references will include an abstract as part of their associated information.

Automatic abstracting is generally considered the preserve of artificial intelligence, as it calls for the manipulation of much real world knowledge. It is more common to find automatic extracting systems which attempt to recognise key phrases or sentences in a document, and then stitch them together to form a (hopefully) coherent extract. Work in extracting is generally undertaken by researchers in information science. Moreover, extracting systems tend to be based on statistical techniques rather than linguistic ones.

1.6.2 Systems which analyse text

Here we single out systems whose primary purpose is to analyse a text, and produce this analysis in a particular form for a particular purpose. This is not to deny the existence of analysis components in other types of system. An MT system has to achieve an analysis before it can transform a text, for example. One sub-type of this class is constituted of systems which apply statistical techniques to yield measures which may then be used to quantify the overall characteristics of a text. Thus word frequency counts, average length of words, sentences, paragraphs, frequency of different grammatical constructions, and so on, can all be used to determine the characteristics of a text. Such systems are typically used to analyse literary works whose authenticity is in doubt, with the aim of establishing whether or not they form part of a writer's works. As they rely more on quantitative techniques, and are by definition monolingually oriented, we shall make no further mention of them here.

There is, though, another type of system which analyses text in a more interesting way (for our purposes), by employing some, cognitive model. Typical applications here are to scan texts for references to particular people or events, and to generate summaries or small resumes concerning these. There is an obvious affinity with automatic abstracting systems, but we choose to make a distinction. Our reason is as follows: an abstract is a text type which has a strictly defined role in information science. It is designed to be a true, condensed repesentation of a document. A story scanner as described above is, on the other hand, oriented towards particular events or prominent people. It is only interested in a text in so far as it contains any information relating to its current preoccupations. Closely allied to story scanners are those systems which produce paraphrases of texts and also summaries. Neither paraphrases nor summaries can be considered as abstracts, though. The systems mentioned in this context are all based on AI principles, and are meant to demonstrate particular points, for example, that a system can be shown to have some kind of understanding of a text. A well-known approach to this relies on Schank's Conceptual Dependency (CD) model. English texts are analysed into a CD network, which is then used as a basis for generating English summaries and/or equivalent summaries in other languages. Although strong claims are made by Schank and his co-workers as to the universality and efficacy of the CD model, severe doubts remain in the minds of the majority of researchers in the field. It has yet to be demonstrated that the CD model is adequate for more than a restricted number or type of texts.

1.6.3 Systems which interact with a human in natural language

As computer systems have become more sophisticated, they have penetrated into more and more spheres of human activity. Although much emphasis is still placed on systems which can handle textual information, there is a growing need for systems which are able to interact intelligently with humans, and which consequently must be able to handle discourse (either spoken or typed) as opposed to more formalised textual information.

This is perhaps the most important area for the field of IT, and certainly that with the greatest potential for growth. As people desire more information, and as the amount and variety of information grows exponentially, so they will have to have recourse to computers to access that information. Computers are no longer the preserve of an elite. People now increasingly expect to communicate with computers without needing special training beforehand. Furthermore, designers of systems now realise that the best method of informing or advising a user is through the user's own language, so-called 'natural language' (NL).

There are many current applications involving such systems, and usually they incorporate some kind of natural language processing (NLP), i.e. some kind of human-machine interaction in NL. These systems go by various names, each referring to a different type of system - Question-answering (Q/A) system, expert system, intelligent knowledge based system (IKBS), etc. Also included here are computer assisted learning (CAL) (or computer assisted instruction - CAI) systems, and speech understanding (SU) systems.

A question-answering system, as its name implies, is designed both to accept queries and to generate answers in NL. It carries on a conversation with a user to determine exactly what information he wants, then extracts this information from its stored knowledge and generates a reply. Q/A systems are fully discussed in Chapter 5.

Expert systems embody the knowledge of several subject specialists in their data bases and can provide expert aid, not only by divulging information, but also by explaining how and why they arrived at some decision, or made some inference. Such systems then act as consultants - they allow a user to explain a problem, and will suggest some solutions, or tests that can be made to provide more information, and give an expert appraisal or judgement. Often, an expert system will perform better than a human expert. However, they are typically used in a consultative role, and so final interpretation of the data, or final decisions, are left to human beings.

A characteristic of expert systems is that they rely on large stores of expert knowledge, which must be acquired somehow. A feature complementing the consultative feature is then the ability to acquire knowledge, or to engage in the transfer of knowledge. This process is not so easy as it may seem, as human experts are not always skilled at expressing their knowledge. Much of their knowledge may be encapsulated in hunches or anecdotes that have their origin in wide experience of the field. It is therefore a non-trivial task to enable an expert system to cull its knowledge from subject specialists. Not surprisingly, a major preoccupation of expert systems designers has been the representation and use of knowledge. Workers in CL have been critical of AI expert system designers in the past, for placing greater emphasis on knowledge repesentation techniques than on NLP, considering this latter to be a relatively straightforward task. Happily, NLP has now been widely accepted in AI circles as a key area for research. We will refer again to expert systems in our analysis of Q/A systems in Chapter 5 and MT systems in Chapter 4.

1.6.4 Computer-assisted learning

Education is becoming increasingly influenced by the use of computational systems designed as teaching aids. From the early days of computing, the basic ability to recognise patterns quickly was exploited to provide CAL systems. Not surprisingly, these had much in common with early MT systems, in that they attempted no more than a crude matching of a student's response to stored ideal patterns or 'answers', using the same techniques as early dictionary-based MT. There was little attempt to analyse a student's responses in order to discover a class of errors, or a class of mastered topics.

Syntactic analysis then became popular, but the old problems of forming a model of the learner's state of knowledge, and of being able to respond intelligently, remained. Since the 1970s, work in AI has had a significant impact on CAL.

A well-known CAL system is SOPHIE, which combines NL analysis and techniques of inferencing. This system was designed to teach electronics students how to detect and repair malfunctions in electronic circuits. The interesting aspect of SOPHIE was that it established an environment for the student to work in. Thus, some malfunction would be generated in the circuit model, and all consequences examined, before the simulation of the malfunction was presented to the student for repair. The student engaged in a NL dialogue with SOPHIE and could detail changes to the circuit, ask for measurements, specify components to be replaced, etc. They could then ask SOPHIE to run a simulation involving the proposed changes and observe the results. Changes to the circuit were examined by SOPHIE, and questions put to the student to make sure that the nature of the malfunction was understood. In contrast to earlier systems, SOPHIE employed a semantic grammar, giving faster and richer results than a syntactic grammar. This is due mainly to the ability of a semantic grammar to avoid generating many nonsensical interpretations, as is common with syntactic parsers. However, SOPHIE can only be used for one narrow task, and it is not possible to generalise this system to handle teaching tasks in other subject domains. As part of the objective of the system was to eliminate meaningless interpretations, this meant that all the objects, processes and actions relevant to the specialised domain had to be uniquely described, and a grammar written to account for all and only these phenomena. Thus SOPHIE, while being good at its particular task, cannot be turned to any other without undergoing major revision.

An early (and continuing) use of CAL, which is relevant to our interest in multilingual questions, was in the teaching of foreign languages. Two recent projects are worth describing.

'The Scottish Computer-Based French Learning Project' is a major project designed to assist the learning of French at anything up to undergraduate level. The system has been piloted successfully in Scottish schools, and is in regular use at the University of Aberdeen. It is based on translation exercise materials, and simulates the competence of a native speaker to check translations proposed by a student. The system does not interrogate the learner, but rather encourages an exploratory attitude, by prompting him or her to try out different translations. There are plans to extend the system to handle other languages.

ELISA is an intelligent knowledge-based tutor for teaching translation skills regarding French and Italian conjunctions in context. The system attempts to build a representation of the student's behaviour which coincides with its correct stored representation of the knowledge required to translate conjunctions in context. ELISA uses this continually updated model to guide its choice of questions to put, until the model of student behaviour matches its own internal one. This approach differs from traditional CAL techniques, as questions are generated dynamically at execution time, according to responses. A session proceeds in two phases – a

straightforward presentation phase, when students get positive
feedback (the correct response) if they fail to answer properly,
followed by an assessment phase, when errors (misconceptions) are
recorded, analysed and classified, then remedied by informing the
student of the nature of any misconception(s). Although developed to
teach the proper translation of conjunctions, the system is amenable
to teaching translation of any word or structure the meaning of which
is context-dependent.

These brief descriptions of current projects demonstrate how
computer-assisted language learning has progressed from the early days
of slot-filling to a concern with establishing models of linguistic
knowledge and models of student knowledge, so that systems may respond
intelligently to learners' mistakes.

1.6.5 Speech understanding systems

The last major area of CL appliation is that of speech understanding
(SU). It is this domain that promises to extend the range of
application of CL systems enormously. With an intelligent speech
processing facility, human interaction with computers suddenly becomes
rapid and easy. More importantly, hands are then freed from the
necessity of typing, meaning computer systems can be used by people
who have their hands full at the best of times (pilots, surgeons,
etc). At present however, unrestricted speaker-independent
understanding is not practicable in the general case. Existing
systems have yet to be demonstrated to perform well under non-
artificial conditions. The major problems of SU are those of
filtering out extraneous irrelevant data from the speech signal
(including background noise) and of dealing successfully with
connected speech.

From the 1960s onwards, isolated word recognition systems have been
developed, which have achieved in some cases high levels of
recognition (over 90 per cent). Today, such systems are readily
available at low cost. Success rates however are markedly affected if
a system is required to recognise utterances by more than one
individual. Usually a system has to be 'trained' afresh for each new
speaker. Neverthless, the performance of certain of these systems is
impressive, and their range of stored vocabulary can be quite large.

Isolated word-based systems are however of limited use. Thus it is
that, since the early 1970s, most research in this area has been
directed towards developing systems capable of understanding connected
speech. Note that there is a fine but important distinction between
speech understanding and speech recognition. Recognition of
individual words does not imply or require understanding. However, it
is widely accepted that successful analysis of connected speech
requires a high degree of understanding. It is therefore not
surprising to learn that SU systems are based on techniques drawn from
AI and CL, and that current research emphasises the integration of
various knowledge sources (acoustic, phonetic, syntactic, semantic,
morphemic, pragmatic, prosodic, stylistic, dialectal, etc.).
Understanding, as opposed to recognition, is an active process, and
involves, for the human, the formulation of expectations as to what an
utterance means, or to how partially completed utterances will

continue. SU system designers have attempted to encapsulate this
process in their systems by employing sets of filters and constraints.
Thus a system may be led at a certain point in an utterance to expect
a certain element, due to the triggering of syntactic constraints
based upon previous context, and will then set up filters to allow it
to ignore extraneous incoming data. This is not to imply that
analysis proceeds in a left-to-right manner. Commonly it does not,
most systems preferring an island-driven approach, where key elements
e.g. nouns are first identified due to their being given clearer
enunciation, and then attempts are made to analyse outwards from these
hopefully correctly identified 'islands'.

1.7 FURTHER READING

Linguistics
Lyons (1981a) is a good introduction to linguistics, and Crystal
(1980) is a handy work of reference. Elementary works on morphology
and syntax include Palmer (1971), Allerton (1979), and Huddleston
(1984), while semantics is covered in Lyons (1981b) and Hurford and
Heasley (1983). For general works on generative grammar, see Lyons
(1977b), Smith and Wilson (1979) and Newmeyer (1983). Generative
syntax is covered in Akmajian and Heny (1975), Radford (1981) and
Newmeyer (1980), and Case grammar in Somers (1985). Rayward-Smith
(1983) gives a clear introduction to formal grammar.

Lexicography
The most recent introduction to lexicography is Hartmann (1983a),
while the standard work is Zgusta (1971).

Computer science
Part I of O'Shea and Eisenstadt (1984) discusses Lisp and another
relevant programming language, Prolog. Zorkoczy (1982) is an
introduction to information technology. Introductions to artificial
intelligence include Boden (1977), Rich (1983) and Winston (1977).

Computational linguistics
Barr and Feigenbaum (1981, ch. 4) and Ritchie and Thompson (1984) are
overviews of work on natural language processing. Book-length
introductions to computational linguistics include Winograd (1983),
M. King (1983) and Tennant (1981). Berwick and Weinberg (1984) is an
advanced work on the relation between computational and theoretical
linguistics.

Current applications
Automatic abstracting is discussed in Paice (1977).
    Text paraphrasers include SAM (Schank and Abelson 1977), PAM
(Wilensky 1977), and DIALOGIC/DIANA (Hobbs et al. 1982). On
Conceptual Dependency, see Schank (1972).
    On expert systems, see Barr and Feigenbaum (1981), Ritchie and
Albers (1983), Stefik et al. (1982), and Lauriere (1982).
    General works on computer-assisted learning include Carbonell
(1970) and Barr and Feigenbaum (1981). SOPHIE is discussed in
Anderson and Kline (1979) and Burton and Brown (1979). The Scottish
Computer-Based French Learning Project is described in Farrington
(1984), and ELISA in Cerri and Merger (1983).
    Lea (1980) discusses the potential of speech-understanding systems,

and Newell (1975) some of the major problems.   A useful source is the documentation of the ARPA-SUR project: Klatt (1977), Lea and Shoup (1980), and ARPA-SUR Steering Committee (1980).

2   Dictionaries and the computer

The contribution that automation can make to dictionary production and use is highlighted by the contrast between the potential of computers and the constraints of conventional printed dictionaries as storage and retrieval devices. A computer has the capacity to store large quantities of data in an ordered yet flexible manner. It can search this stored data quickly and select and combine parts of it in order to meet a diversity of specific information needs. A conventional dictionary can be regarded as a large collection of data ordered in a particular way. However, because of the inherent immutability of the printed page, the structure and organisation of a conventional dictionary are highly inflexible and not always appropriate for all its users. Moreover, consulting a dictionary is time-consuming and frequently complex, as a user does not normally require all the information found under one entry but rather selective quantities from several entries.

The advantages of using computers to assist in the production of dictionaries were recognised early on and are now widely exploited by dictionary publishers, compilers and users. With the growth of developments in hardware and software, methods of using computers for lexicographical purposes have become more sophisticated. Starting from the imitation of human work methods and of conventional forms of dictionary presentation, the properties and scope of computer technology have been exploited to promote improved methods of compilation, new forms of dictionaries, and new ways of using them.

In order to present the full range of issues involved and in the absence of many detailed reference works to recommend to the reader, this chapter examines the nature of conventional dictionaries (2.1), the diverse functions of the existing variety of dictionary types and their structural characteristics (2.2) as a prelude to the discussion of the new possibilities and changes in lexicography facilitated by the application of automated techniques (2.4).

While many of the issues presented in this chapter are not discussed in explicit connection with multilingual dictionaries, in fact most are relevant for lexicography in general, whether mono-, bi-, or multilingual. Indeed, in so far as dictionaries can be said to be constructs in a semi-artificial language which serves as the interface between 'real' (natural) language and the items of reality to which natural language refers, all lexicography is in some sense 'multilingual'. Nevertheless, there are certain issues which are salient in, or exclusive to, bi-/multilingual lexicography in the more usual meaning of the term; these questions are examined separately (2.3).

2.1 THE NATURE OF CONVENTIONAL DICTIONARIES

Just as a full understanding of issues in machine translation requires
an awareness of the linguistic and methodological problems involved in
the activity of human translation (cf. Chapter 4), so the field of
computational lexicography (see section 2.4) is best examined against
the background of its manual precursor. We therefore begin by
outlining the main features of traditional lexicography, in order to
highlight its limitations and thus explain the appeal of automation
and its potential to enhance efficiency at every stage of the complex
lexicographic process.

2.1.1 The dictionary as text type

Dictionaries constitute a particular type of text which is distinct in
both form and function. At a formal level, their most distinguishing
feature is their limited syntax characterised by a lack of linguistic
connectivity and the absence of metalinguistic or situational
discourse. The basic lexical units (headwords), the entries and their
parts are related only by sequential, horizontal and vertical ordering
supplemented by various numbering and typographical devices, the
interpretation of which is explained in a separate section, often the
preface. The particular mode of presentation chosen is determined by
two factors: the compiler's perception of the organisational structure
inherent in the data and, more crucially, the dictionary's intended
function, i.e. its target user group.

The formal, linguistic characteristics of conventional printed
dictionaries render them in many ways closer to texts in an artificial
language than natural language texts and thus make them particularly
amenable to computerisation. However, the application of automation
to lexicography is not simply a question of making existing printed
dictionaries machine-readable but rather of exploiting the
capabilities of computers in order ultimately to change the very
concept of dictionary itself. This new conception of dictionaries
would be based on the enhancement of their role and mode of use in an
environment free from the formal constraints of a physical two-
dimensional medium.

From a functional point of view, a dictionary, like a textbook, can
be said to be a didactic tool. However, whereas the knowledge
gleaned from a textbook may be widened and deepened by repeated
reading and can be accessed without prior knowledge of the book's
structure, the consultation of a dictionary is a singular, selective
operation which requires at least some degree of familiarity with its
organisation and conventions. In contrast to other text types, the
dictionary declares - often in the preface, or else by convention - a
particular pre-established structure and order of items of reference
which is fixed for the entire document. This repetitive pattern of
dictionaries accounts for the distinctive way in which they are used;
they are seldom read from cover to cover but are referred to at
different times according to specific needs. The organisational
rigidity imposed by the printed page is ill-suited to accommodate such
a process of selective consultation (see 2.1.2), the ease and
efficiency of which would be considerably enhanced by the application
of automated storage, search and retrieval techniques.

Finally, it is important to remember that dictionaries are also distinguished by their special social status as authoritative reference tools, the impact of which is essentially evaluative. Any listing of words entails selection (because, except for concordances of individual texts, it can never be exhaustive) and ordering, both of which imply prior evaluation. Inclusion as opposed to exclusion, the selection of one pattern of pronunciation over another, the listing of, say, five rather than seven meanings for an entry all represent evaluation. A dictionary is consulted for the preferred meaning, recommended pronunciation, deviant spelling, etc. To this extent it can be said to be an acknowledged arbiter of language and language use, a fact which makes it incumbent on lexicographers to endow their products with the coverage, consistency and reliability which are appropriate to this influential role.

2.1.2 Limitations of conventional printed dictionaries

The ability of conventional printed dictionaries to fulfil their established authoritative role has been prejudiced by their singular inadequacy as a means of representing lexical data. This inadequacy stems partly from the inherent constraints of the printed page but is also due to a long tradition of lexicographical conservatism.

The fundamental challenge for lexicographers has been to cope with the sheer size and dynamism of the lexicon (see 1.3). The collection of lexical data is a monumental task, and the accurate representation of such open-ended, constantly evolving phenomena in a closed, static system is virtually impossible. Lexicographers can thus never be satisfied that a dictionary is complete or even up-to-date. The quality of a dictionary has become a matter of balance between the number of entries and the amount and type of information about entries. The massive quantity of lexical data and the diversity of information that can be provided about them has led to the production of an increasing number of separate types of dictionaries which may be classified according to subject field, type of information given, etc. (see 2.2.1). This diversification of dictionary production has gone some way towards rationalising working methods by making it possible for lexicographers to deal with more manageable amounts of data. However, the market has continued to demand – and economic viability has necessitated – the production of single-volume, multifunctional dictionaries, compiled from massive resources of lexical material, the collection and classification of which require a huge investment of time and personnel.

The inefficiency of traditional working methods is compounded by the more fundamental constraints of the printed medium itself. From an organisational point of view, the biggest and most obvious drawback of printed dictionaries is the alphabetic ordering of entries which separates and so obscures the associations between lexemes that are related semantically or grammatically. A particularly problematic issue – and one often cited by lexicographers – is the need for a consistent treatment of multi-word units or compounds. Their relationship to the individual lexemes of which they are constructed can be treated alphabetically only at the expense of reduplication of entries (compare, e.g. petrol pump, off the record). Yet it might be highly desirable for certain user groups, e.g. foreign language learners, to be aware of important productive patterns of compound formation. For example, the common practice of placing nominal compounds formed according to the object-verb pattern in English (e.g. <u>trout fishing</u>, <u>horse breeding</u>) into the entries of the corresponding verbs makes the task of retrieving the compound difficult for the user who is unfamiliar with such techniques. While some dictionaries have tried to break away from such constraints and adopt an organisation based on conceptual classifications (which, in any case, has its own drawbacks), alphabetisation has remained a key lexicographical principle. Even pronouncing dictionaries and spelling dictionaries follow the alphabetic order and hence direct from written form to sound.

Conventional dictionaries are further restricted by their layout. There are some generally agreed conventions for European languages, e.g. left to right ordering, indentation, top to bottom ordering, a hierarchy of punctuation marks, etc., but they are on the whole insufficient to represent the variety and structure of information categories required in dictionaries. Typographic conventions, in particular, have contributed to certain ambivalences of information categories which create considerable problems of interpretation. Further, since dictionaries are forced to present information in a highly concentrated way, they do not specify a full set of information categories for every entry. The user therefore has to draw on past experience to infer from a complete entry information which is missing from another. Economising on space thus results in increased effort for the dictionary user; in the case of, say, a foreign language learner, it may even block or at least slow down the process of consultation.

2.2 TYPES AND STRUCTURES OF DICTIONARIES

The information given in dictionaries varies considerably and gives rise to numerous different types of dictionaries intended for various user groups and needs. Many types of dictionaries contain the same basic information but differ either in the order in which this is given or in the amount of detail presented in each information category. In this section, we present a brief classification of dictionaries and discuss the way in which the information they contain is structured.

2.2.1 Classification of dictionaries

The number and variety of conventional printed dictionaries is constantly increasing as user requirements become more diversified. Because of the multiple functions of most dictionaries, the range available cannot be neatly subdivided into clearly distinct types. However, dictionaries can be classified along several dimensions, such as:

1 <u>Means of organisation of entries</u>. Entries may be ordered alphabetically (the practice in most conventional dictionaries) or conceptually (as in e.g. thesauri).

2 <u>Intention</u>. The degree of prescriptiveness in dictionaries may be more or less pronounced (see 2.1.1 above on evaluation).

3 <u>Aspect</u>. Dictionaries may exhibit a synchronic or a diachronic approach. The former attitude is exemplified in dictionaries of contemporary usage, the latter in etymological or historical dictionaries.

4 <u>Mode of presentation of information</u>. Information may be given statically or dynamically. The tendency of many dictionaries to present entries as collections of static items of information fails to meet the needs of those users (e.g. foreign students of a language) who require a dynamic presentation of information which illustrates the potential of the lexicon, i.e. the language not only as it is, but as it can be. Geared towards such users is the monolingual pedagogical or learner's dictionary which is characterised by the prevalence of explanations, and a full use of contexts and examples.

A major difficulty for the compiler of a learner's dictionary is the assessment of user needs. The lexicographer needs to know, for example, which items and processes present most learning difficulty for users and which they consider most important. The assessment of user requirements is a generalised problem in lexicography since market research on dictionary use is not widely practised. Interestingly, this is another area in which computers can play a significant role: once users have direct access to data bases (see below), their needs and preferences will be easier to monitor and the current necessity for compromise and guesswork reduced.

5 <u>Specificity of lexical data</u>. Dictionaries may further be distinguished according to whether they deal with the elements of general language, i.e. the general, 'everyday' lexicon as used by an entire language community, or special language(s), i.e. a subset of the lexicon of a language (or languages) which contrasts with general language by being restricted in its use to one or more socio-professional groups. However, the borderline between general and special language cannot be rigidly defined. Words cross over freely from one side to the other; technical words pass into general usage as the knowledge they represent becomes popularised (e.g. <u>software</u>, <u>bit</u>) and general 'everyday' words often acquire specialised meanings (e.g. <u>heat</u>, <u>noise</u> in physics). The fluidity of the divide between general and special language creates problems for dictionary makers on both sides. The general lexicographer has to decide which technical words are sufficiently 'everyday', i.e. established in general usage, to merit inclusion and which special meaning(s) of such words should be given. The special lexicographer, on the other hand, faces such questions as whether to include information on the syntactic structures characteristic of (but not exclusive to) a special language and, more importantly, how to delimit the boundaries of the special subject area(s) to be covered.

Over recent years, the demand for special dictionaries has grown steadily. Moreover, this demand comes from a wide range of users, including scientific and technical experts and students,

professional translators, technical writers and the interested
layperson. This variety of demand, coupled with the continual
diversification and increasing complexity of scientific and
technical knowledge has contributed to the development and
proliferation of term banks, which have helped to overcome many of
the problems of specialised/technical lexicography. (See Chapter
3 for a detailed discussion of developments in this area.)

6 Nature of information. The ratio of linguistic to non-linguistic
(encyclopaedic) information provided in dictionary entries varies
considerably. Technical dictionaries are likely to contain a
higher proportion of conceptual information (in the form of
detailed definitions, illustrations, etc.) than the everyday
general dictionary. However, commercial demand for a practical,
multi-purpose reference tool has fostered an increasingly
preponderant encyclopaedic element in the latter.

7 Number of languages. In this respect, three broad types of
dictionary can be distinguished: monolingual, bilingual and
multilingual. Although the fundamental problems and processes are
largely the same for all dictionaries, it is nevertheless true
that the number of languages included in a dictionary has a
considerable influence on its content and presentation. This is
most notable at the level of semantic information. Since this is a
central issue, we discuss it separately in section 2.3 below.

The many possible permutations and combinations of the various
features described above produce a great diversity of specific types
of dictionaries. Indeed, the market has been inundated with
dictionaries ranging from the one-volume, general-purpose, 'family'
dictionary through various technical dictionaries to the many
different specialised (or speciality) products such as reverse
dictionaries, frequency dictionaries, dictionaries of neologisms, of
proper names, of idioms, of slang, etc. The range of available
dictionaries is impressive but most types are only sporadically
produced; in practice, the general dictionary prevails in printed form
and, because of commercial considerations, is increasingly multifunctional. The contribution of information technology to lexicography
lies in its ability to facilitate the production of infinitely many
specific dictionaries in a variety of formats without sacrificing
commercial viability.

2.2.2 Dictionary structures - the lexical entry and its parts

The lexical entry is the basic structural component of a dictionary.
In conventional, printed dictionaries, it takes the form of a
paragraph consisting of a headword followed by an enumerated set of
information categories or specifications.

The headword is the most crucial element of the dictionary since it
is the key to all information. Most dictionaries are lexeme-based
(see 1.3 for an explanation of the notion of 'lexeme') and give as
headword the graphic form of the lexeme which, if necessary, is
subdivided, e.g. first according to word category and then according
to its semantic scope.

A common set of specifications or entry categories is as follows:

1 A phonetic specification, indicating the lexeme's pronunciation.

2 A graphic specification, including spelling variants (e.g. regional, diachronic).

3 Morphological and syntactic specifications. These vary considerably according to the purpose of the dictionary and range from a simple indication of word category (e.g. noun, verb, adjective, etc.) to more detailed typological information on word categories (e.g. transitive/intransitive, mass/countable, etc.). For variable word categories such as nouns, verbs and pronouns, an indication is usually provided as to whether inflections are predictable according to a general rule, or irregular. A common criticism of these specifications is that they reveal a rather naive linguistics on the part of the lexicographer.

4 Semantic specification. It is the nature and amount of semantic information that is the greatest source of diversity among dictionaries. Probably the most striking contrast is between monolingual and bi/multilingual dictionaries. The general monolingual dictionary usually gives the meaning(s) of a lexeme (by synonym, definition or example), a synonym or related lexemes and usage information. (Monolingual specialised dictionaries often use definitions only.) In bi/multilingual dictionaries, on the other hand, semantic information centres on the notion of equivalence, which we examine more fully in section 2.3.

5 Pragmatic specification. This may be provided indirectly through the inclusion of examples of usage, or indirectly via register labels (e.g. 'colloquial', 'slang', 'archaic').

2.3. BI/MULTILINGUAL DICTIONARIES AND THE NOTION OF EQUIVALENCE

Zgusta defines a bilingual dictionary by declaring its 'basic purpose' to be

> to coordinate with the lexical units of one language those lexical items of another language which are equivalent in their lexical meaning. (Zgusta, 1971, p.294)

The basic principle underlying bilingual dictionaries is thus that of interlingual semantic equivalence. This book is not the place for a discussion of the theoretical validity of this principle; that would take us far beyond the scope of this chapter into the fields of lexical semantics and translation theory. Nevertheless, since the application of this principle has repercussions at all stages of the lexicographic process (see 2.4 for a breakdown of this process), it is appropriate to examine in detail its practical implications. We restrict our discussion to bilingual dictionaries, but the notion of equivalence is equally relevant in multilingual dictionaries which can seen as dealing with multiples of language pairs. To emphasise this point, we use the term 'interlingual lexicography' to cover both bi-

and multilingual dictionaries.

2.3.1 Translational and explanatory equivalence

Broadly speaking, two types of equivalence may be distinguished: translational equivalence and explanatory equivalence. A translation(al) equivalent Y of a source language (SL) entry word X is a lexical unit which coincides in meaning with X and can be directly inserted into a sentence of the target language (TL). So, for example, the French item garçon is the translational equivalent of boy. An explanatory equivalent, on the other hand, cannot always be inserted into a TL sentence; it explains or describes the meaning of the SL word. Thus, the French explanatory equivalent of the word boyhood might be état de garçon, but this could not be used as a translation equivalent; for this, an alternative designate such as jeunesse would be used even though this fails to capture the semantic restriction of the English word, since it is neutral with respect to sex.

The distinction between translational and explanatory equivalence is, however, far from clear-cut - indeed, the two concepts can even overlap. Translational equivalents may be either absolute, that is, they may coincide exactly with the entire grammatical and semantic range of the lexical meaning of the SL word, or partial. Absolute equivalents are extremely rare, due to the phenomenon known as anisomorphism, that is, the differences between the conceptual systems of different languages and the corresponding divergences in the organisation of their lexicons. The nature and extent of the divergences between different language pairs gives rise to varying levels of partial equivalence. Some instances of partial equivalence are due to interlingual lexical ambiguity, i.e. variations in the lexical richness of different languages in certain semantic fields. (See section 4.4.1.1 for a discussion of this problem in the context of machine translation.) Here, the lexicographer is faced with the problem of mapping one lexical item onto many equivalents. Examples of this phenomenon abound: consider, for instance, the English noun river which has two possible translation equivalents in French, rivière and fleuve, the respective semantic fields of which only partially coincide with that of the English item. The way in which the lexicographer tackles this sort of problem depends in part on the directionality of the dictionary, that is, whether it is intended for a French or an English native speaker. The notion of directionality is a key factor in determining questions of content and presentation in bilingual dictionaries.

The existence of culture-specific or culture-bound words, i.e. words which denote concepts or objects that are peculiar to one linguistic community also poses problems for the interlingual lexicographer. Examples of this are legion. Consider Spanish bodega, French tutoyer, English pub, to mention but three well-known ones. Of course, there are degrees of culture-specificity; some words are more culture-bound than others. The Polish word choina (a record of a person's property in the land registry) is thus clearly more culture-specific than tutoyer. The degree of culture-specificity of an item determines whether the lexicographer gives a translation equivalent, an explanatory paraphrase, something in between the two, or both. Thus,

<u>tutoyer</u> is given the following entry in <u>Harraps New French and English Dictionary</u> (1972):

> to address (s.o.) as 'tu' or 'toi' (instead of 'vous'); to be on familiar terms with (s.o.)

Only the second part of this entry can be considered a translation equivalent; the first is clearly an explanation and could not be used in an English translation.

Usually, interlingual lexicographers aim to provide both a translation equivalent and an explanation for culture-bound items. (A notable exception was the important lexicographical theoretician, Scerba, who advocated the principle of absolute predominance of the translation equivalent and would not admit explanations in his dictionaries.) However, in some cases, it may be necessary for the lexicographer to create a translation equivalent specially for the purpose, often by borrowing the expression from the SL, either wholesale or adapted to the TL linguistic patterns. The following is an example, taken from Smirnitskij and Akhmanova's Russian/English Dictionary (1948/77):

> <u>essentuki</u>: essentuki (kind of mineral water)

In the extreme case, it is impossible to give a translation equivalent, for example, in the case of onomatopoeic words for which only an explanatory gloss can be provided. Zgusta (1984, p.149) quotes as examples of this the following two entries from Lambrecht's <u>IFUGAW-ENGLISH Dictionary</u> (1978):

> <u>hukhuk</u> ... onomatopoeic word used by gamblers when they shuffle the cards
>
> <u>uga</u> ... squealing of pigs

Before concluding this section, we should mention specialised/technical interlingual lexicography in which the problem of equivalence is reduced to some extent by the emphasis on precise definitions. Nonetheless, the existence of competing schools of thought, and terminological deficiencies in the languages of societies which are not technologically advanced means that the problem is not entirely obviated (see Chapter 3 and further reading below).

We have seen that the content and organisation of interlingual dictionaries is determined by their directionality and by the more fundamental problem of anisomorphism. However, the purpose to which the user puts a dictionary has equally important implications for its structure and presentation, which we discuss in the next section.

2.3.2 The aims of bilingual dictionary users: production vs. comprehension

Essentially, a user consults a bilingual dictionary for one of two purposes: to translate from their own language L1 into another, L2, or to translate from L2 into L1. The first of these aims is called production (or encoding), and the second comprehension (or decoding). Given these two purposes and the fact that we must deal both with speakers of L1 and speakers of L2, four types of bilingual dictionary emerge:

For L1 speakers:

1 A production dictionary in which the entry words are L1 and the target language is L2;
2 A comprehension dictionary in which the entry words are L2 and the target language is L1.

For L2 speakers:

3 A production dictionary in which the entry words are L2 and the target language is L1;
4 A comprehension dictionary in which the entry words are L1 and the target language is L2.

The information included by the lexicographer, e.g. the nature of the equivalents and the type and amount of grammatical information will be different in each of 1 - 4. Clearly, someone using a dictionary for production purposes will generally require more detailed morphological and syntactic information on the TL than someone using it for comprehension. Other aspects which will vary include the language in which directions (details of typographical conventions, etc.) are given, the selection of vocabulary, the orientation of explanations, degree of cultural information, etc. However, the impact of commercial considerations is such that, in practice, the two types of dictionary for each group of speakers are combined into one dual purpose volume.

It will by now be apparent that the constraints and difficulties of monolingual lexicography are not only mirrored in interlingual lexicography, but augmented by the task of constructing acceptable equivalences between the lexical units of languages which may differ radically in their conceptual and lexical structures. In the next section we set out to show how the introduction of computers into this traditionalist field has helped to reduce these problems.

2.4 COMPUTATIONAL LEXICOGRAPHY

The term computational lexicography refers to the automation of lexicographic tasks. It should be pointed out that this covers a range of possibilities, since today's lexicographers are in a position, notwithstanding financial constraints, to choose the extent to which they wish to involve the computer in their work. They may

merely exploit its ability to perform certain basic operations (e.g.
alphabetic sorting, reference checks, error search, updating, string
manipulations) more quickly than a human without changing the
fundamental organisation of the overall lexicographic process. Or
they may wish to increase the level of computer involvement to a point
where the very nature of the process and its products are profoundly
altered. There are thus different levels of computer integration in
the lexicographic process which all come under the rubric
'computational lexicography'. Drawing an analogy with machine
translation (see section 4.2), these include 'computer-aided
lexicography' where the computer serves merely as an electronic
amanuensis in an otherwise traditional process, through 'human-
assisted lexicography' where the greater part of the work is performed
by the machine, to the still futuristic situation of fully automated
lexicography where the machine has the finesse to perform those
subtler lexicographical tasks which can currently only be carried out
by humans.

2.4.1 Levels of computer involvement in the lexicographic process

The lexicographic process may be broken down into several stages:

1 preparation - data collection and validation;
2 consolidation - data collation and storage;
3 compilation - entry selection and construction,
                 dictionary production;
4 consultation - dictionary use.

In the following sections, we examine the contribution that computers
can make at each of these stages to improve the efficiency of the
lexicographic process as a whole.

2.4.1.1 Data collection and validation

The first and most fundamental stage of the lexicographic process is
the collection of lexical material. Lexicographers are well aware of
the scientific unacceptability of their traditional methods of data
collection. Until large quantities of text could be made machine-
readable and before the availability of computer power and appropriate
linguistic techniques to analyse these data, lexicographers had to
rely on their own observation or that of informants for the selection
of entries and associated information. Now, the development of
techniques of automatic text analysis - though these have yet to be
perfected - facilitates a more objective approach and permits the
establishment of large corpora of attested lexicographic data. Work
on automatic speech recognition, which is still in its early stages,
may lead to analogous corpora of samples of spoken language. In this
section, we are only concerned with written texts.

For years, one of the main impediments to the use of computerised
techniques in lexicography was the high cost of converting printed
texts into machine-readable form. Nowadays, however, publishers
increasingly rely on automated composition techniques; books,

newspapers, journals, parliamentary reports, and many other types of literature are now prepared for printing in machine-readable form and stored in this way for future reference. Today's lexicographer therefore has a wide variety of machine-readable texts available for use as lexicographic corpora. Optical character recognition (OCR) equipment enables these texts to be scanned rapidly and it is even possible for one machine to recognise not only different font styles but also most alphabets. The Kurzweil Data Entry Machine (KDEM) recently made it possible for a 250,000 word corpus of English journalistic texts to be set up in just four weeks (see Knowles, 1984). The Cambridge Ideo-matic Encoder can scan non-alphabetic scripts like Chinese and hybrid scripts such as Japanese (see Nancarrow, 1981).

The advantages of basing a dictionary on a substantial corpus of machine-readable text which testifies to the existence of lexemes and which exemplifies their meaning and use are obvious. The selection of entries can now be justified scientifically, if necessary by frequency of occurrence; fixed objective criteria can be established for obsolescence, and the lexicographer can be supplied with a full range of occurrences of a word from which to choose examples.

The use of corpora of texts also provides criteria for resolving the difficult borderline between general and technical dictionaries. Using a computer, it is possible to produce concordances (see below) or glossaries of, say, one or several textbooks and to annotate a lexical data base so that highly specific subsets of the lexicon can be made available to narrowly defined groups of users. A progression is therefore possible from a single text vocabulary to a vocabulary based on a selection of the texts of a subject field to a general technical or scientific dictionary.

A dictionary based on a corpus further permits a reliable attribution of subject, usage and stylistic labels and, of course, their regular revision. It is possible to trace the introduction of new lexemes or lexeme combinations in a language, the transition from a technical term to a general word (e.g. satellite, acid rain), the adoption of a product name as the generic for the type of product (e.g. hoover, sellotape) or the meteoric rise and fall of a vogue word (e.g.hip, the adjective, and bread, a noun meaning 'money').
For the purposes of data collection, it is also necessary to distinguish between running text and data which are already in a format suitable for lexicographic use. Dictionaries, glossaries, etc. can be converted into machine-readable form, or, if they are already machine-readable, can be entered directly into a data base. With running text, it is necessary for the lexicographer to extract lexicographically relevant data. The automatic extraction from running text of such data proceeds in stages. The first of these is a simple listing of strings of characters between spaces. Such lists provide information such as the relative frequency of occurrence of the various words in a text and the total number of words (the tokens) as opposed to the number of different words (the types). Type-token ratios provide information about the 'density' of texts while the frequency of occurrence of items is a useful objective criterion for the selection of dictionary entries or indeed of vocabulary for use in specialised textbooks.

If a word list takes the form of an index or concordance, it situates the occurrence of a string of characters in a segment of text - a line, a paragraph or page. The lexical unit can be related to the context in which it occurs, for such purposes as verification of homography, disambiguation or exemplification of usage. In such cases the lexicographer will prefer a KWIC index (KeyWord in Context) which lists the word together with a number of preceding and following words. A number of standard concordance 'packages' exist (e.g. the Oxford Concordance Program, OCP) which permit users to specify several processing options, e.g. length of preceding and successive texts, elimination of function words, etc. Concordances are also a source of information on the semantic range of lexical items which can be used to construct definitions although it remains the task of the human lexicographer to select semantic interpretations.

The lexicographic usefulness of such lists and indexes is restricted since homographs are not distinguished and inflected forms of the same paradigm are separated by being listed at different points in the alphabetic sequence. This defeats further statistical analysis and may even confuse the lexicographer. Any further use of text-based listings of lexical items requires the grouping of types and the selective analysis of tokens. The notion of type must be widened to include morphologically related items so that it is possible to get from text items to dictionary items. In addition, lexicographically irrelevant material can be eliminated by the introduction of a stop list which permits the filtering of unwanted words. Thus, for example, the computer can eliminate items such as articles and pronouns which, while being necessary for documenting usage and collocations, are not required for frequency counts or homography detection. This filtering out of superfluous material reduces the indexes to more manageable proportions.

A stop list is itself a word list and its use introduces the principle of comparing lists. This can serve a variety of lexicographic purposes. For instance, text-based lists can be compared with one another in order to determine their relative coverage of vocabulary or they can be compared with a dictionary in order to identify its lexical gaps. A similar technique can be used to produce a special subject dictionary by, for example, establishing a list of the words in a sample of text chosen as being representative of a special subject and then subtracting from this list all those words which also appear in general and other specialised texts. The attribution of special subject field labels in general dictionaries and the representativeness of the vocabulary selected can be validated by checking the occurrence of labelled words in an index of specialised terms. Frequency counts of specialised vocabulary items can also aid the lexicographer to ensure the relevance and currency of such entries in general dictionaries: indexes of new texts are compared to existing ones in order to find new items which have not so far been recorded in the dictionary or words which may have increased their frequency of occurrence and therefore become eligible for inclusion.

Another technique used in text analysis is lemmatisation, the goal of which is to reduce morphologically related forms to a single lemma or stem for dictionary look-up. So, for example, conjugated verb forms are linked with their infinitives, inflected nouns with the

singular subject case, and inflected adjectives in languages with
adjectival agreement for gender and number with the neutral, singular
form. The success of automatic lemmatisation techniques and the
extent to which its results require human post-editing depends on the
language in question.

Lemmatisation programs typically comprise three components: a
lexicon, a set of rules and a filter. The lexicon contains stems,
i.e. free morphemes (e.g. walk, violin, French grand) and affixes,
i.e. bound morphemes (e.g. -er, -ist, French -e/s); the set of rules
governs the possible combinations among the two kinds of lexical
elements; the filter would take the form of a checklist which serves
to reduce the number of phenomena covered by the other two
components. However, the high instance of morphological
irregularities and/or homographs in certain languages prevents
absolute accuracy despite the use of checklists and special homograph
recognition routines. Consider a lemmatisation program for English:
if, for example, the computer is instructed to strip off the final -s
from English verb and noun forms, it should also be capable of
recognising the alternative -es ending, as in glasses, and of
realising that the -s in alms and ethics is not a plural ending. And,
of course, there will always be cases which the programmer has not
foreseen. As yet, automatic lemmatisation rarely achieves 100 per
cent accuracy and very few languages have been subjected to these
techniques. Nonetheless, such programs do provide valuable assistance
to the lexicographer, though the day when the computer can make the
decision of what to include in the dictionary is still in the distant
future.

2.4.1.2 Data collation and storage

> It is no idle exercise of the fantasy to imagine the big
> computerized lexicographic centers of the future where every
> change in the lexicon is registered and richly documented
> ... and which will serve as the source for all studies of the
> lexicon and all compilations of dictionaries of the
> respective languages. (Zgusta, 1971, p.355)

Zgusta's prophetic remark foresaw the revolution in the work of
collating and storing lexicographical data thanks to the development
of computerised data base techniques. For centuries, these tasks were
performed manually as teams of lexicographers laboriously recorded
information on index cards to build up massive filing systems which
took decades to produce and were difficult to maintain. The sheer
volume of data to be treated was such that many ambitious dictionary
schemes were abandoned or forced to make compromises in size or
quality. The introduction of computers and, in particular, the
exploitation of data base management systems (DBMS) have provided
lexicographers with an efficient, flexible means of handling massive
quantities of information and, indeed, have had such an impact on
their work that the concept of a lexicographical data base can now be
said to have superseded the dictionary as the predominant working
concept in lexicography.

If the task of a lexicographer can be considered as that of building a data base, a totally new methodology can be introduced which is both more economical and more flexible. A data base approach permits lexicographic work to be an on-going activity in which decisions about data to be collected are taken quite independently of decisions about dictionaries to be produced. Previously, lexicographers had to have a very clear idea of their future dictionary's layout and purpose before deciding which data to record. This obviously slowed down work, cut out options and increased the margin of error. Within a data base approach, given a properly planned housekeeping system, unlimited development of records and files is possible while preserving the option of making available to the user an almost limitless variety of output formats so that virtually no user request need be refused. Dictionary consultation can also be planned to satisfy user needs which could not be met before or which were not known to exist. Like other branches of the information industry, lexicography can now usefully undertake both product and market research since the traditional product can be diversified (see below).

A further advantage is that an on-going data base can cope better with the essential dynamism of the lexicon of a language than any traditional, inherently static dictionary. It can monitor the development of a lexical item from its creation onwards by recording any subsequent change in its meaning, etc., and when a form or a meaning become obsolete. It is now perfectly feasible to construct a comprehensive data base for any one language, to add to it, to reduce it, and to modify entries or parts of entries with ease. In this way, massive collections of data are built up that mirror the lexicon of a language and from which dictionaries can be extracted for particular purposes.

A number of languages already possess the material for a comprehensive lexical data base in the form of files for a large national dictionary. One example is the Trésor de la Langue Française which was begun in 1960. Described as 'perhaps the most ambitious historical-period dictionary project' (Merkin, 1983, p.129), it is based on a computer-generated archive of 90 million quotations taken from a thousand texts (all of these having been processed in seven years) and an Inventaire général de la langue française (1820- 1920), a collection of six million quotation slips.

Similarly, in Britain, the entire text of the 1933 12-volume edition of the Oxford English Dictionary is currently being entered into the computer. The four volumes of the Supplement (the final one of which is due to appear in 1986) will be integrated and the resulting integrated OED is scheduled to be published at the end of 1987. The electronic version of the OED will have a wide range of applications. A questionnaire was circulated by the heads of the project (a collaborative venture between the University of Waterloo, Ontario and Oxford University Press) with the aim of determining those facilities most likely to be required by users. Among the many possible facilities envisaged are the following:

- queries on words, including, for example, requests for the English vernacular equivalents of Latin plant names or for all interjections in common use in a certain period;

- queries on word meanings, such as requests for the metaphorical uses which a particular author makes of words, or for all terms from a certain subject field the definitions of which contain a certain string;

- queries on related terms, e.g. for all terms related to a certain place over a certain historical period.

Creating a lexical data base of this sort is a costly and time-consuming enterprise. Commercial publishers do not normally have the resources to plan on sufficiently large a scale, though data bases exist for an increasing number of medium sized general dictionaries which have considerable growth potential and flexibility for producing subtypes (discussed in the next section).

Furthermore, lexical data bases have overcome the impediments to data access created by the principle of alphabetical organisation which obtains in conventional printed dictionaries, machine-readable dictionaries and dictionaries on magnetic tape. By abandoning the alphabetic sequence a lexical data base can provide direct and differentiated access to the various data categories it contains and so offers multiple approaches to the same data (see next section). The lexicographer can store a record of information consisting of the main data field, typically the definiendum or dictionary headword, and associated sub-fields, namely the data categories contained in a typical dictionary entry.

Given that the record of a lexical entry can have up to twenty data categories in any one language, there is a considerable accumulation of information in a data base. Some of the data categories refer to parallel or different fields in other entry records, e.g. synonyms, cross references of words used in definitions or examples so that a network of inter-record relations is created. Whereas traditional printed dictionaries had to enter such cross references individually, computers can automatically generate pointers from one record to another. Thus the complex network of relationships is constantly maintained in the data base; all that is required for their selective output are criteria by which some are made overt in particular subsets, to provide e.g. dictionaries of synonyms, antonyms, etc. The data base with its many relationships between records is therefore both a mirror of the lexicon and a knowledge structure in its own right.

2.4.1.3 Compilation

The new possibilities of large machine-readable corpora and lexicographical data bases have improved dictionary making and use in many ways and new techniques are constantly being developed. The advantages of basing entry selection on substantial corpora of machine-readable text are manifold: the choice of entries can be justified scientifically, objective criteria can be established for obsolescence, register labelling, subject field attribution, etc., and a full range of occurrences of entry words are available for the purposes of exemplification (see above).

However, it is the adoption of data base techniques for the storage and management of lexicographical data which has been the key to the revolution in dictionary making. The main advantage of these techniques is that they allow 'the multiple use of stored entries in many different ways' (Vollnhals, 1984, p.433). To give readers an initial idea of the significance of the lexicographical data base philosophy, we quote a contemporary academic lexicographer who writes that it is:

> powerful and flexible enough to encompass everything from the major, highly-structured, explanatory or bi/multilingual dictionary, replete with systematic information, ... via the hierarchically and tightly-structured information-science thesaurus or the semantic dictionary of terms arranged according to their distinctive feature configurations ... to the lowly crossword-solver's companion, denuded of all information apart from its listing structure. (Knowles, 1984, p.309)

Lexicographical data bases can, on the one hand, be used to produce conventional printed dictionaries more cheaply, more quickly and, above all, more frequently or, at the other end of the scale, they can help to change the very nature of dictionary use by allowing direct, on-line consultation by users. Between these two extremes, they facilitate several intermediate possibilities in dictionary compilation which are distinguished by, for example, the physical realisation of the product (e.g. book, magnetic tape, disk, chip), or its degree of permanence (e.g. volatile information displays of information vs. hard copy printout).

Leaving aside the question of the physical characteristics of data base products, we shall look at the ways in which data base techniques promote the diversificaton of lexicographical products in terms of content and presentation without prejudicing – and, indeed, even enhancing – cost-effectiveness. Later, we shall focus specifically on the implications of data base philosophy for multilingual lexicography.

The techniques of data storage and management in a data base offer diversified access to lexicographical information and retrieval of this information in a variety of differently structured formats. Broadly speaking, output facilities may be of three types: 'one-off' listings for individual customers tailored to suit their particular requirements; a wide range of lexicographical products with a broader commercial appeal; and information derived on-line. At present, the amount of individual, custom-built lexicographical products is limited and tends to prevail in specialised lexicography (i.e. term banks, see Chapter 3). On-line use is also restricted but will doubtless become increasingly prevalent (see 2.4.1.4). Currently, therefore, the main application of lexicographical data bases is to enhance the diversity of products with a broad potential commercial appeal.

A lexicographical data base may be regarded as a structured collection of records containing information which is divided up into fields (see 3.2.1). If we consider a lexicographical data base record to correspond to a lexical entry in a dictionary, its main data field would be the entry headword while the associated sub-fields would contain those items of information given in an entry's specifications (e.g. phonetic specification, register label, definition, morphological and syntactic specifications, etc. - see 2.2.2). Other sub-fields may contain additional information which is not normally found in a conventional dictionary such as date of input of entry into data base, sources, etc.

The main difference between a lexicographical data base record and a conventional dictionary entry concerns their structure. A conventional dictionary entry is organised linearly; relational information is expressed implicitly in the form of presentational and typographical conventions. Furthermore, the format and length of an entry are largely determined by economic constraints. A lexicographical data base record, by contrast, contains information which is formalised and highly structured, and the relationships among fields and records are expressed explicitly. The size of records is determined by considerations of storage capacity and cost, but the use of pointers to generate automatic cross-references makes this far more efficient than in a rigid printed format. While the records each have an internal structure, they - or certain fields thereof - are also related to associated records or fields of other records. These 'external' structural relationships which organise the data base are constantly updated and maintained. Information is thus stored in many dimensions; it is the possibility of selecting and combining any number of aspects of any number of dimensions which explains the enhanced versatility of output.

To give the reader a more detailed idea of this versatility, we shall consider some of the options available using selection programs and their possible applications.

One option would be to select all records in the data base containing a certain value for a certain field, or a combination of such values and to output the results of the search as a simple word list. So, for example, one could request all those records with the subject field value 'physics' and receive as output all physics terms contained in the data base. Similarly, a request for all records in which the value of the stylistic register field was 'slang' would yield a dictionary of slang expressions.

Alternatively, one could request as output a more complex listing containing not only words but also some associated information, i.e. the values of a particular field or fields. Such a listing would thus serve as a mini-dictionary. In this way, one could, for instance, request all headwords together with the value of their phonetic transcription and thereby receive as output a pronunciation dictionary. A synonym dictionary could be obtained by requesting all headwords and the value of their synonym field. A simple defining dictionary would be the result of a request for all entry words and the contents of their definition field.

The number of possible output formats obtained by requesting different permutations of the information contained in data base records is vast. (For further illustration see section 3.6.2.) If one takes our exemplification to extremes, one could easily imagine requests for highly specialised groups derived by combining several search dimensions. Such a request could yield, for example, a glossary of eighteenth century tin mining vocabulary used in Cornwall and still in use, or a list of currently obsolescent electrical engineering terminology.

The extent of the versatility afforded in a data base approach should by now be obvious. It should perhaps be reiterated that this flexibility in data storage and management has beneficial implications for lexicographers throughout the various stages of their work. No longer are they required to have a precise idea of their future dictionary at the outset of a project; nor, indeed, are they limited to one dictionary project at a time.

> The computer .. makes it possible, in a really major way, for the lexicographer to keep all his options open all the time. It is possible to apply different foci to lexical data bases, once assembled, in a manner which does not pre-empt future projects. In other words, the computer ensures the maximum data potential. (Knowles, 1984, p.309)

An ideal beneficiary of this guarantee of 'maximum data potential' is the historical lexicographer. Indeed, since about 1950, large-scale historical dictionary projects have relied increasingly on computer-generated archives, containing millions of quotations, thereby allowing for the flexible extraction of small-scale lexical archives from one large data base of historical information.

Finally, one crucial benefit of automation to the commercial lexicographer is that it speeds up the rate of production. Not only are dictionaries published more quickly, they are also published more frequently. The end product is thus more up-to-date and so more reliable. A representative of one large Danish publishing house recently remarked that the new technology had

> radically changed the way in which we produce dictionaries and lexicons by enabling corrections to be made more cheaply, more easily and more quickly. (Norling-Christensen, 1982, p.214)

To illustrate this, he points out that whereas in the past economic constraints meant that dictionaries were only revised every twenty to thirty years, now revisions were appearing every two to three years. Similarly, automated production techniques made it possible to publish a ten-volume lexicon in just 13 months; before the use of such techniques, the maximum production figure was two to three volumes per year. The experience of this publishing house is only one of many examples of commercial ventures to have been revolutionised by the advent of technology.

The advantages of enhanced efficiency and productivity we have discussed apply of course to all dictionary projects. However, there are some aspects of automation which are particularly useful for multilingual lexicography. One striking example is the way in which recent developments in software and hardware technology have facilitated multilingual output, one of the most obvious problems to be solved. Some software and printing firms have developed programs for bilingual output (on a line printer, VDU and photocomposing unit) using Roman and Arabic character sets with diacritics (see e.g. Ehlers, 1982). Similarly, it is now possible to create bilingual dictionaries on-line using such technological advances as bilingual screen terminals and laser printers (see Busharia et al., 1982).

But the contribution of computer technology to bi/multilingual lexicography goes beyond the possibility of printing multiple character sets. In addition to the feasibility of producing a variety of more specialised types of bi/multilingual dictionaries without endangering commercial viability, there is also the question of generating multilingual dictionaries from monolingual data bases. However, this process is by no means straightforward. As our discussion of the problems of equivalence and anisomorphism indicates, the idea of just integrating and 'matching' two or more monolingual data bases to create a bi/multilingual dictionary is simplistic in the extreme. Each separate meaning of an entry word in one language may be represented by a different entry in another or not be acknowledged at all. Moreover, the requirements, and so the characteristics, of mono- vs. bi/multilingual dictionary entries differ fundamentally. Thus, for example, a monolingual dictionary is definition-oriented, whereas a bilingual dictionary takes definitions for granted and concentrates on usage (based on the various meanings established by the definition) and on providing equivalents (often for phrases rather than individual words) particularly for those meanings of an entry word that offer potential difficulties in translation. Further, it is usually more explicit with regard to usage, the collocation of items and the grammatical behaviour of items in both languages (an exception to this being the specialised, technical dictionary where the range of usage is predetermined).

Nevertheless, a monolingual data base can be seen as a convenient starting point for the creation of parallel data bases for the production of bi/multilingual dictionaries being enriched by many examples of context required to demonstrate the range of appropriate target language equivalents. (See e.g. van Sterkenburg et al., 1982.)

Finally, one very specific contribution of automation is towards the more efficient production and use of multilingual glossaries. The consultation of these glossaries, which include as many as six languages, is unwieldy and complex, and may involve several different pages and index numbers for any one required item of information. The automated production of such works would facilitate greater flexibility for the user as well as offering clear advantages for their compilers, since the formulation of these glossaries requires a rigorous system of indexing and cross-referencing, both of which processes are performed far more quickly and efficiently by a computer.

2.4.1.4 Consultation

While the main contribution of automation to lexicography has been to enhance the versatility of its products, it has a more radical

implication, namely to change the nature of dictionary consultation.
This is manifested in two ways: first, it introduces the possibility
of direct, on-line consultation, thereby freeing users from the
practical constraints of printed media; second, it allows users to
access one very large store of information equivalent to the sum of
many conventional dictionaries in a variety of ways.

The idea of dictionary users working directly at a terminal is by no
means a futuristic one, although it is yet to become widespread
practice. In some commercial enterprises, however, (e.g. Siemens, see
section 3.8.4) it is already the norm for translators to work on-line,
consulting a dictionary data base according to their needs without
having to leaf through several unwieldy reference works. Moreover, a
wide range of text processing facilities is now available (see section
4.2.1) which offer users a variety of labour-saving options, e.g.
'paging through' a data base on-line, split screen devices, etc.
These advanced working methods have been shown to improve both the
productivity and quality of translators' work. (It has been reported
that conventional dictionary look-up can take up to 60 per cent of a
translator's time. The use of computerised aids such as text-oriented
glossaries can increase a translator's productivity by 50 or 60 per
cent and reduce their error rate by 40 per cent - see Sager and
McNaught 1981b, sec. 5.4.)

Probably the most important advantage of lexicographical data bases
is the possibility of direct and differentiated access to data. The
principle of alphabetical organisation no longer reigns supreme; users
are offered multiple approaches to the same data according to search
criteria (e.g. morphological, syntactic, semantic) which are
linguistically more relevant and thus likely to be of more interest
than any based merely on the alphabetic sequence. Access to keywords
is already - or soon will be - possible on the basis of pronunciation,
approximate spelling, constituent elements from a definition or even
from an image. Moreover, the possibility of accessing combinations of
information hitherto unobtainable can often lead to

> new discoveries of linguistic facts which are almost
> impossible to achieve in the conventional printed versions.
> (Nagao et al., 1982, p.52)

The significance of this technological advance is most striking in the
context of the distribution of information by telecommunication
networks. It is clear that a large market exists for
'teledictionaries', although several problems have to be resolved
before the so-called 'telematics revolution in lexicography'
(Reichling, 1982, p.266) can be fully realised. Among these is the
controversial issue of copyright and the need for international
agreement on some standardised method of data exchange (see section
3.7).

2.5 SUMMARY AND FUTURE TRENDS

The electronic revolution has now been in progress for a number of
years in lexicographical publishing and has done much to improve

productivity and efficiency and to diversify the range of dictionaries available, thereby enhancing their commercial appeal. The use of computers to assist in the preparatory stages of data collection and collation speeds up the overall production process and relieves the lexicographer of the tedium of routine tasks. The flexibility afforded by data base management and storage techniques facilitates the publication of a wider variety of lexicographical tools which are more reliable since they can be frequently revised and updated. The user is thus offered a greater choice than ever before, not only in the range of products but also in the way in which these are used. While the scope of on-line consultation is as yet limited, its expansion is a realistic prospect.

However, despite the undoubtedly significant contribution of computers, the advent of fully automated lexicography is still in the distant future, as the following quotation points out:

> It would be a great mistake, however, to think of the computer as a potential simulator of a dictionary editor's behaviour. The intellectual tasks entailed in dictionary-making, such as researching the meaning of terms in different languages, will remain the province of man now and for some time to come. (Vollnhals, 1984, p.431)

The computer cannot perform exacting analytical tasks, which often require human intuitions and subtle judgement, but it can handle huge amounts of data in a short time and make them more manageable to use. For the foreseeable future, then, it will remain a tool and not a substitute for the human lexicographer.

In addition to the inherent intellectual shortcomings of the computer as lexicographer, the wholesale automation of the lexicographic process is further impeded by the restricted availability of hardware. While computers have been shown to be of economic benefit, the capital outlay required for the purchase of hardware and training of appropriate personnel remains, for the time being at least, prohibitive.

Finally, there is the need to re-educate dictionary users. Just as traditionalist lexicographers have to revise their attitudes and update their working methods, so must users be weaned away from the conventional modes of dictionary presentation and consultation. However, there are clear signs that this re-education is already in progress.

Looking to the future, the prospects for computational lexicography are exciting. As the capabilities of computers continue to be refined, their contribution to lexicography will no doubt increase so that the traditional notions of dictionary production and use are changed still further. One interesting possibility is that of compiling orthophonic dictionaries with phonetically based entries for the day when humans can converse orally with computers. Such innovations, together with the likely future use of telecommunication lines direct to the home could create a new concept of a personal dictionary consultant.

2.6 FURTHER READING

The nature of conventional dictionaries
In addition to the two standard reference works, Zgusta (1971) and Hartmann (1983a), we also recommend for selective reading two sets of conference proceedings, Hartmann (1979) and Hartmann (1984).
For a discussion of the contrast between natural language and artificial language see Sager et al. (1980), sec. 3.5.1. Text types are discussed in ibid., Ch.6.
Cowie (1983a) examines some of the difficulties facing lexicographers in trying to accommodate the recording of grammatical information with the organisational constraints of conventional dictionaries.

Types and structures of dictionaries
See Zgusta (1971), chapter V for a general discussion of dictionary types.
Readers interested in specific classes of dictionaries can consult the following articles which cover most of the illustrative classes mentioned in this chapter:
Merkin (1983) is an interesting paper on historical dictionaries which gives a chronological account of their development with many examples.

Various aspects of the learner's dictionary are discussed in Cowie (1983b, 1984) and Moulin (1983).

Hartmann (1983b) describes one of the few research projects on dictionary use, which surveyed the use made of bilingual dictionaries by British learners of German. See also Hatherall (1984) and Bejoint (1981).

For discussions of dictionaries for special registers, see Opitz (1983).

Zgusta (1971), ch. VII discusses the bilingual dictionary. For a discussion of the construction of dictionary entries see Zgusta (1971): sec. 6.5 (monolingual) and 7.7 (bilingual).

Bi/multilingual dictionaries and the notion of equivalence
Zgusta (1971) deals with this in his sections 7.1 and 7.6.
See also Al-Kasimi (1983) for a discussion of two major problems for interlingual dictionaries: the selection of ready equivalents and meaning discrimination.
Snell-Hornby (1984) discusses the inadequacy of the notion of equivalence. Translational equivalence is explored in Zgusta (1984) and in Tomaszczyk (1983, 1984) (the latter two articles being particularly interesting for their discussion of the notion of culture specificity).

Computational lexicography
For selective reading, consult Goetschalckz and Rolling (1982), a collection of papers on current developments and issues in the field, and Hartmann (1984), Part III.
For more information on computer-produced word lists see Siliakus (1984). Those interested in finding out more about the OCP should consult Hockey and Marriot (1982).
Olsson (1982) discusses the issue of copyright in relation to

electronic publishing.

Summary and future trends
The notion of the orthophonic dictionary is examined in Lurquin (1982).

3 Terminological data banks

3.1 INTRODUCTION

Today, almost all industrialised nations have set up, or are in the process of setting up, terminological data banks (henceforth referred to simply as term banks) which provide a wealth of information and services to many different types of user. The development of term banks may be said to derive from various contributing factors. These include the proliferation of terms, advances in computer science, the growth of the information industry and particularly of information science, the increase in the number and diversity of users of terminology (and especially of multilingual terminology), the widespread dissatisfaction among users with traditional lexicographic tools and the development of terminology as a recognised discipline.

The proliferation of terms due to advances in science and technology is occurring at an exponential rate. Conceptual systems, especially in the newer, more volatile areas of knowledge, are becoming more and more complex. Traditional methods of recording and storing terms have proven inadequate to cope with this complexity, being both slow and, if not rigorously carried out, open to inconsistency. Moreover, the amount of cross referencing within a terminological system, and between it and neighbouring systems, and further between these and conceptual systems of other languages, imposes a heavy burden on traditional methods in a world in which fast, efficient retrieval of relevant data is the overriding concern.

The previous chapter presented some of the products of conventional terminological lexicographic research which are available to users, namely specialised dictionaries, glossaries, thesauri, etc., in mono-, bi- or multilingual form. The rate of terminological evolution in certain subject areas, however, is such that many of these traditional lexicographic works are either outdated or incomplete by the time of their publication. They are also expensive to produce, bulky, time-consuming to use and prone to wear and tear.

Computers have made a significant contribution to terminological lexicography through their capacity to perform quickly and efficiently such tasks as data collation, sorting, merging, etc., thereby facilitating speedy and more reliable production of specialised dictionaries. However, there are two aspects of the process which remain essentially unchanged: the method of compiling dictionaries and the actual format of the finished product. An inflexible, pre-defined presentation of terminological information is of limited general usefulness and makes severe demands on the time and patience of users who are often required to chase up several cross references during the consultation of a single entry. Term banks, by contrast, present users with a multiplicity of specialised tools and allow them to manipulate, search, cross reference etc. the stored data with ease, and without any knowledge of the processes involved. The ideal term bank allows users to define their own search strategies and output formats, so that only such information is received as is pertinent to the users' needs. Term banks are thus more user-oriented, and likely to replace conventional printed dictionaries in the long run. In addition, they can be used to produce a larger variety of printed dictionaries geared to different user types. It is therefore likely that publishers will increasingly organise their dictionaries as data bases which can be continuously updated, and from which relevant subsets of information can be extracted at any one time to produce a particular custom-built type of dictionary.

Most term banks were originally set up for one particular purpose only, but at present there is a move towards a wider scope and more general functions. The main functions of a term bank are the collection, processing, storage and dissemination of terminology. These tasks are pursued for three main reasons:

1 to enable the user to produce better quality work, notably when the user is a translator;
2 to enable users to work more efficiently, by giving them rapid access to accurate, up-to-date terminological information;
3 to control neologisms and harmonise existing usage.

3.2 STRUCTURE OF TERMINOLOGICAL DATA BANKS

3.2.1 Fields, records, data bases and data banks

A record is a data structure comprising one or more fields, each of which represents a unit of information. A term record represents the core information relevant to a terminological datum, i.e. a term or phrase etc. It contains fields to represent, for example, the term/phrase itself, its definition(s), synonym(s), translation equivalent(s), explanatory or defining contexts, etc. Other fields may indicate abbreviations, pronunciation, grammatical information, subject classification, quality codes, sources, keywords, conceptual relationships to other terms, the author of the record, and the date of composition (see 3.5.) The number of fields per term record varies considerably from one term bank to another, ranging from as few as six to as many as 76.

A data base record may be thought of as akin to the 'acquisition record' filled out by a terminologist. However, they are not identical. The data base record may represent the information of the acquisition record differently; it will also contain additional information to allow the computer to establish its own cross-references for retrieval purposes. It is rare that a whole record is the subject of a retrieval operation. Search procedures normally interrogate individual fields or groups of fields, and output only a fraction of the sum of the information about a term, namely that specified by the user. Thus, in contrast to a printed dictionary, users will be shown only those items they wish to see, with no spurious or distracting information.

A data base is a structured collection of records, in the sense that it represents the relationships between the records. In our case, these will be mainly terminological relationships, and the data base will thus represent, for example, the concept system of the terminology of a particular subject field. One computer may handle several different data bases, any set of which may be interrogated, or combined or split for various purposes. A certain amount of redundancy may also be tolerated, with some records appearing in more than one data base, entering into similar or different relationships with their neighbours. Usually, though, the contents of different data bases are taken to be separate and disjoint.

The term 'data bank' is used to refer to a collection of data bases, together with the associated hardware, software and personnel. It is a stock of information, plus the means of accessing that information. It is to be noted that the terms 'data base' and 'data bank' are often used imprecisely in the literature; indeed, their meanings are interchanged in some authoritative works.

3.2.2 General components of a data bank

(This section provides an introductory overview of data bank architecture and may be omitted by the knowledgeable reader.)

At the heart of the data bank lies the computer, consisting of the central processing unit (CPU), which may be programmed to perform specific tasks, and the central (or main) memory, to which the CPU has direct access, and which may be used to manipulate data structures and to temporarily store currently activated programs. The set of programs is controlled by an operating system, whose commands allow the various utility programs required for data processing to be activated (reading, sorting, file maintenance, output to peripheral units, etc.). Advanced data banks implement a high-level query language, which may be a more or less restricted form of natural language, and which allows the user to access the data bank without having to master the sometimes complex commands of an operating system. The main feature of a data base query system is that the users do not realise that they are programming a computer.

The computer communicates with the data and the outside world via a number of peripheral units. These include auxiliary storage devices capable of holding large amounts of data (magnetic tape, hard disc, etc.). Today, there are term banks containing a million term records and an average record length is some 300 characters. Thus off-line storage for such a bank would need to cater for 300 megacharacters. In addition, storage space will be needed for the various thesauri, indices, and search files which the computer uses to speed up its search and which, in a conventional data bank, will take up much more room than the data. By comparison, the main memory of a computer is considered large if it can contain one megacharacter. Other peripheral units include the input and output devices which permit man/machine and machine/machine communication - visual display units (VDUs), printers, photocomposition units, microfiche equipment, optical character recognition devices (OCRs), modems, etc.

44

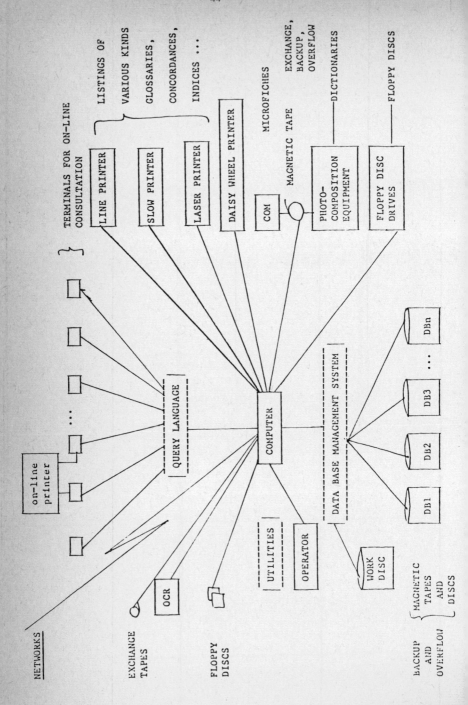

3.2.3 Architecture of a term bank

Figure 3.1 represents the architecture of a general purpose term bank, designed to serve many different types of user, in ways adapted to their needs, and to provide many different, flexible lexicographic tools. This diagram is idealised to a certain extent as it takes no account of, for instance, distributed processing, possibilities on microcomputers versus mainframe processing, techniques of associative processing, etc.

It is important to stress that a term bank is much more than an automated dictionary of concepts and terms. It is rather to be seen as an exhaustive collection of terminological data whose scope is that of an entire library of specialised lexicographic works. The extreme flexibility in combining, formatting and selecting from these data afforded by the computer means that a wide range of tools and services in the form of custom-tailored information can be provided. A term bank permits users to be selective, allowing them to specify how much and which type of information they want. Many modern term banks have 'packages' designed so that, for example, a translator will receive a different collection of information from, say, a standards expert.

The true term bank frees the user from the need to consult separate dictionaries for different special subjects or different types of dictionaries for different kinds of information, e.g. a definition, translation equivalent or synonym. It also guarantees that the retrieved data will be up to date, appropriate to the context and of reliable quality.

An interesting application of term banks is their use in on-line systems in which they are linked to text-processing equipment to allow, for example, a translator to display the source text in one 'window' of a VDU, the target version in another, and terminological information culled from the term bank in a third. At least one large term bank (TEAM, see 3.8.4) has automated this process so that the translator is given a source text with an interlinear display of target language equivalents determined by the term bank, which the translator may then accept or reject. The full potential of term banks has not yet been realised, however. New methods of consultation and of data display and use are continually being implemented.

3.3 CLASSIFICATION OF TERM BANKS

It would be futile to attempt a complete description of existing, individual term banks: they are constantly increasing in number and are experiencing such rapid expansion and technical development that any description would be out of date by the time it appeared in print. Such a detailed treatment would, in any case, be beyond the scope of this book, for the purposes of which it is sufficient to characterise term banks according to general criteria.

Term banks can be classified on the basis of a number of criteria of which the following are probably the most important:

1 Objectives. Term banks may have the goal of circulating Scientific and Technical Messages or STMs (as in for example translation and preparation of texts), distributing terminologies (for dictionaries and the teaching of Language for Specific Purposes or LSP,) or standardising or harmonising terminologies (language planning). These aims often overlap, however; while the original motivation for the creation of term banks was largely monofunctional (e.g. for translation in the case of TEAM), their objectives have diversified over the years so that they are now multi-purpose tools.

2 Users. Term banks may also be classed according to the users for whom they are intended. These include translators, terminologists and terminological lexicographers, technical writers (conference interpreters, writers preparing textbooks, etc.), specialists in scientific or technical subject fields, information scientists, LSP teachers and the general public. (See further section 3.6.)

3 Attitude to language. While some term banks (e.g. NORMATERM) include only standardised data and thus may be said to have a normative or prescriptive attitude to language, others are purely descriptive and include data of all types without value judgements. Falling between these two approaches is the informative attitude where non-standardised data are included but with value judgements attached, e.g. EURODICAUTOM.

4 Nature of data. Whilst all term banks contain by definition terminological data, they incorporate to a greater or lesser extent data of other kinds, viz. documentary, translational (e.g. concerning context of use, conceptual correspondence between two equivalents in different languages), linguistic (morphological, syntactic, orthographic, encyclopaedic, lexical (general language) and visual (diagrams, illustrations, etc.).

5 Organisation of data. The data in a term bank may be organised by language into bi- or multilingual relationships; they may also be organised conceptually according to systematic relationships among entries.

6 Method of distribution. Broadly, methods of distribution of terminological data contained in term banks fall into two categories – direct (i.e. on-line via local or remote terminals), and indirect (i.e. off-line via a high speed printer, computerised typesetting, teletype or telephone). However, it is common for term banks to practise a variety of distribution methods since a flexible approach to output and access enhances their cost-effectiveness.

In practice, these criteria are variously combined into several types. Brief descriptions of some major term banks are given in 3.8 below; in each case we seek to focus on a particular approach or feature of interest which distinguishes the bank from others.

3.4 THE COLLECTION AND PROCESSING OF TERMINOLOGICAL DATA

Preparing a term for input to a term bank involves gathering all information on the term necessary for completing each field of the term record (see next section). In practice, however, only certain information is available, or it has been decided to record only partial field information in order to attain quickly a workable level of records with minimum information in any one subject field. This means that the term record will be updated later.

The most important source of data is the term bank's own team of terminologists who extract terms from STMs in various subject fields or, when necessary, create new designations. Before the data thus produced can be incorporated into the term bank they must be verified and converted into machine-readable form.

The second most important source is contributions from outside the term bank, e.g. from a terminological committee, a major expert in the field, or, increasingly, from another term bank. Inter-term bank exchanges have so far been infrequent, because of the problems of compatibility which arise, less at the technical level than at the level of the terminological content. (This question will be discussed in section 3.7.)

The third source is the users of the bank: translators, technical writers, subject specialists, LSP teachers, abstractors, etc., who may contribute the terminological information which they encounter in the course of their work. Unfortunately, this source is not generally as productive as might be expected, principally because users consider the recording of detailed information on terms too difficult and time-consuming.

Discovery of new terms can be substantially assisted by using an automatic aid such as the MTR (Multilingual Terminology Recognition) system of the International Telecommunication Union.

If new data arriving from outside are already in machine-readable form, they will be quickly incorporated in a term bank; otherwise they will have to be input manually, a process which is naturally more time-consuming. Data coming from other term banks will have to be transferred to the in-house record format, while data originating from regular contributors may be expected to be in the required format, if for example a network of contributors has been organised, each member having the capability to record data in machine readable form. Data originating in the term bank itself will normally be input on-line, into the desired format. After a certain period, a substantial collection of data will exist, held in a special data base, or file, i.e. in a subsection of the term bank. It will not yet be part of the main data bank, although it will have been controlled for quality. This file will then be sorted via various programs which will produce, for example, an alphabetically ordered file, check that record numbers or term numbers are consecutive, check that record fields and record lengths have been respected, etc. At frequent intervals, say every fortnight, this file of data will be merged with the old master file, and a new master file, plus backups, produced. This new master file will undergo further checks, and be divided into the various subject areas. Inversions will be generated (e.g. elements of multi-terms will appear as main entries) as will synonym entries (i.e. terms appearing in the synonym fields of a record will appear as main entries). This last procedure greatly increases the number of search terms available. After a last series of checks the old data base will be replaced with the new.

All entries should be subject to rigorous quality control, as quality and reliability are the most important features to customers. At regular intervals, or following a policy decision or complaint, an entry will be subject to updating, which involves changing, adding or deleting information. This may involve parts of fields, whole fields or whole records, the objective being to allow optimum access to current terminology.

What has been described here is a relatively idealised data input and validation methodology for a term bank. While each term bank has its own methods and procedures, the general process is the same for all.

3.5 TERM BANK RECORD FORMAT

The design of the term record format is crucial to the overall effectiveness of a term bank. Considering the multifunctional requirements of a modern term bank, it is reasonable to suppose that a term record should include the following fields:

1 Record identifier (e.g. record origin, term number)
2 Record originator
3 Date of record input or updating
4 Language/country code
5 Entry term
6 Source of entry term
7 Note on usage
8 Grammatical information/quality code
9 Scope note
10 Full synonyms
11 Abbreviated form
12 Synonyms
13 Conceptual link (pointers to generic, specific, associated terms)
14 Subject field
15 Definition
16 Source of definition
17 Context
18 Source of context
19 Foreign language equivalent(s)
20 Source of foreign language equivalent(s)
21 Foreign language equivalent note on usage
22 Foreign language equivalent scope note
23 Foreign language equivalent context
24 Foreign language equivalent source of context

It is to be noted that the schema outlined above assumes a bilingual term record format; certain fields would reduplicate in a multilingual record. It is also possible to have a term record which is conceptually organised which would imply a different format again. Moreover, some fields will contain fixed length, fixed content information, e.g. 3, some will contain variable length, fixed content information, e.g. 5, others will contain variable length, variable content information, e.g. 7. Variable length and variable content fields are required also for special purposes, for example, implementation of another language, or for incorporating specific data when manipulating data for publishers, registering keywords, descriptors, etc.

3.6 USERS AND USER FACILITIES

3.6.1 User groups

A recent study determined the existence of six main groups of people who would regularly use a term bank (Sager and McNaught, 1981a). These are:

1 Technical writers, abstractors, journalists, translators and interpreters – the largest group, having in common that they are professional communicators, working on behalf of others to mediate linguistic messages. All the members of this group regularly need to verify the meaning and establish the appropriate usage of specialised expressions and to find equivalents for them in other languages.

2 Information and documentation specialists (librarians, indexers, information brokers) who require information on existing terminology so as to identify documents reliably, and to construct thesauri for classification and document retrieval purposes.

3 Standardisation experts, a small and highly specialised group who are increasingly publishing glossaries of standardised terms to designate uniquely and unambiguously the objects of their standardisation efforts.

4 Specialist lexicographers and terminologists who serve all the other groups, collecting and recording existing usage in special subject fields and advising on new usage. The growth in the number of term banks means that these functions may be carried out more efficiently and on a much larger scale than ever before.

5 Applied linguists, language planners, researchers in machine translation, LSP teachers and educationalists, who require vocabulary listings, statistics on frequency of usage, core vocabularies of special subject fields, etc.

6 Dictionary publishers who require the service functions of a term bank to store and manipulate large corpora of linguistic data.

In addition to these regular users, there are a number of other groups of diverse backgrounds who would benefit from access to a term bank on an intermittent basis. Such users might, for example, wish to use a term bank monolingually to check the existence, spelling or definition of a term or expression. They may also use it bilingually to help them read a technical foreign language text or to obtain a specially compiled glossary to write a research paper in a foreign language or attend a conference conducted in a foreign language with which they are reasonably familiar. Examples of such users are:

1 A customs official checking the documentation accompanying imported goods; there is no time to check various specialised dictionaries, and often a term is too recent to be found in a dictionary anyway.

2 Members of Parliament visiting foreign countries needing a selective glossary to understand explanations or written material.

3 A manufacturer who needs information on terminology pertaining to products intended to be sold in a foreign market.

4 An insurance agent who deals with claims in a very specialised field.

Each of these groups requires different types of terminological lexicographic tools and displays of information, although some of these requirements overlap to a certain extent. However, while there is a move towards an increase in scope and functions, the difficulty of keeping pace with evolution of terminology and of coping with large volumes of input data means that term banks do not provide satisfactory responses to all possible queries. The potential is there, however, for term banks are tending to specialise in certain areas, and are entering into data exchanges or data networks to provide users with access to other subject areas. At present, some term banks attain 75 per cent success rate in particular subject fields; a more general average would be in the 50-60 per cent region.

3.6.2 User facilities

In order to cater for the diversity of needs of the various types of user, it is necessary for a term bank to provide a variety of output formats. Search operations and query procedures must therefore be as flexible as possible. Here we present a simplified and rather idealised view of user facilities in order to avoid entering into confusing detail on the many services and query languages which are available. The reader should, however, be aware that while some term banks have most, if not all, the facilities we describe, others have only a subset of them.

3.6.2.1 Search facilities

It seems reasonable to suppose that a pre-defined common set of search operations will be suitable for all user groups. These would enable the user to search on the following:

1 a term, that is, a defined sequence of characters, a single-element or multi-word term;
2 an arbitrary string, to ask, for example, for all terms beginning with, or containing, a certain pattern;
3 an abbreviation;
4 a list of terms, where information common to all terms in the list alone is required.

Operations on 1 and 3 involve specific field searches, as opposed to general field searches. All of the above can be made available both in off-line and in on-line mode.

In addition, 'paging' through the data base is usually available in on-line mode. Three types of paging are common:

1 paging in the alphabetic order of the SL or TL;

2 paging in the systematic order of the SL or TL, (i.e. following conceptual links);

3 paging through successive multi-word terms beginning with or containing the query term.

These manual search operations can be supplemented by automatic means, so that if a query term has not elicited a match, the computer can be instructed to widen or deepen the search. It is possible, for instance, that a single-element query term only exists as part of a larger multi-word term. The computer could then automatically further the search and offer, for example, multi-word terms containing the query term on the principle that some information may be gleaned.

The computer can also be programmed to search for elements of multi-word query terms by searching the synonym field; alternatively, if in on-line mode, the computer may be programmed to ask the user to specify a synonym. In order to widen a search, terms can also be truncated by the user or automatically. Such an operation may incorporate morphological principles, or be merely brute mathematical truncation.

3.6.2.2 Output formats

It would be impossible to enumerate in full the range of output formats available to users since there are many combinations involved. Some of the common options are:

1 a complete term record or certain fields thereof. The user can either specify their own sets of fields to be output or use pre-defined sets; e.g. two or three 'standard' or general purpose sets defined with a view to the needs of particular user groups.

2 selected fields of more than one term record, output in the form of:

(a) monolingual alphabetic indices, giving e.g. term and generic term;

(b) bilingual/multilingual indices giving e.g. term, synonyms and translation equivalents;

(c) text-oriented lists in which terms are output in the order they occur in a text together with the fields desired, e.g. term, translation equivalent, source;

(d) alphabetic/systematic lists or glossaries, by subject area(s), by language(s), by project(s), by source(s) giving e.g. term, definition, hierarchic relations, antonym;

(e) phraseological glossaries;

(f) concordance/indices;

(g) full-scale dictionaries;

(h) linguistic thesauri, giving e.g. hierarchic relations and synonyms.

The real superiority of a term bank over the conventional dictionary resides in the ability of the computer to perform intelligent searches combining search fields of related records. Such operations are not only desirable for widening the search but can also be exploited for identification of a term in relation to other similar terms. The computer can, for instance, automatically generate clusters of related terms. This technique takes advantage of hierarchical classification, being based essentially on the superordinate-subordinate relationship. (See Sager and McNaught, 1981c, sec. 3.3.2)

Output is normally available via a variety of media:

1 visual display unit, ranging from screensful of information to single lines. Screen 'windows' may be used: for example, one part of the screen may contain the query term and numbers of records in which the term appears; another part may contain individual field information, and another may be reserved for consultation of source documentation. A window of a user's own terminal may be reserved for text-processing, and term bank information appear in a second window; hierarchic displays may also be output. The user may therefore choose, according to needs, from a variety of output formats;

2 hard-copy (off/on-line printer, telex);

3 microfiche - the format (fields, number of columns, etc.) would be decided by the user;

4 magnetic tape, complete with control characters to drive e.g. publishers' photocomposition equipment. In the case of a dictionary, users could define their own entry format including the typographical conventions of published dictionaries;

5 floppy disks - for use by users' own systems, containing subsets of the term bank and, if required, subsets of complete term records.

3.7 EXCHANGES AND COOPERATION BETWEEN TERM BANKS

It would scarcely be feasible for a term bank to attempt to include every concept and every term in every subject field in the hope of achieving a response rate close to 100 per cent. Ideally, therefore, subject fields should be subdivided among all term banks and standardised methods of processing and storage established in order to guarantee the interchangeability of the terminological data.

Over recent years there has been a move away from, the original perception of term banks as individual entities with separate objectives and particular user groups towards the incorporation of banks into data networks. Such networks may assume three forms:

1 an exchange network, involving term banks and various terminology centres wherein data are collected and exchanged on a large scale;
2 public information networks, where term banks are made available for large-scale public (international) access e.g. EURONET-DIANE and SCANNET;
3 private partnership networks as with, e.g., Siemens.

Networks and exchanges notwithstanding, it would appear that term banks will remain relatively specialised in certain fields.

There are of course a number of political and economic factors which influence and limit the scope of exchanges and other forms of cooperation. Nonetheless, the growing mass of terms to be listed, classed and distributed, and the practical impossibility of a single bank processing every term means that a bank must eventually seek international exchanges in order to respond more satisfactorily to the specific needs for which it was created.

Since each term bank has its own specific objectives, it also has its own criteria for selecting the data to be processed, as well as its own methods of collecting, storing, processing and distributing terminological data. Consequently, there will inevitably be considerable gaps and overlaps in the choice of data in the different term banks. While, objectively speaking, the terminological reality is always the same, each term bank emphasises a particular aspect of this reality according to the needs of its intended users. None of the existing banks use the same system of classifying terminological data, and their methods of classifying supplementary documentary data may also differ.

Implicitly or explicitly, every term bank assigns two types of relative value to the data it contains: an internal relative value based on a standard within a language and a comparative relative value measuring the quality of the conceptual equivalence between two or more terms in different languages. The criteria for internal relative values may vary considerably from one bank to another. Moreover, not all term banks are equally interested in assigning comparative relative values, that is, a rating indicating the quality of the correspondence between a term and its equivalent.

The diversity of existing term banks is deeply rooted and inevitable. The solution to the problem of exchanges between term banks cannot come, in the short or medium term, from any modifications in their internal structure but lies rather in a means of transfer of data which does not affect this. What is needed, then, is a measure of agreement among banks regarding the status of terminological data. In other words, exchanges would be possible under two sets of circumstances: either banks agree to store terminological data in a format which has a common interpretation (which is idealistic), or they agree on an exchange format. This latter option, which is the more feasible, requires each bank to develop two pieces of software, one to convert their data into the exchange format and one to transform received data into their own data structures. The actual, physical exchange could be carried out using MATER (see 3.7.2); however, what is crucial is to have agreement on the interpretation of the content of the data fields.

3.7.1 Technical aspects of the transfer of terminological data

Attempts have been made in the past to transfer terminological data from one bank to another and to integrate the data thus received into the stock of the receptor bank. The experiment was attempted, for instance, in 1974, between the term banks of the University of Montreal and the European Commission in Luxembourg. Subsequent study of the operation has shown that a considerable investment of time and effort was required on the part of the receptor bank's computer staff to integrate the Canadian data.

In the meantime, experiments with data exchanges have shown the need to devise a separate exchange format for lexicographic and terminological data which does not affect the internal structure of the banks participating in such an exchange. An exchange format on magnetic tape has been developed by the International Organisation for Standardisation, ISO, for bibliographical data. A parallel international standard is also now available for terminological and lexicographical data (see 3.7.2).

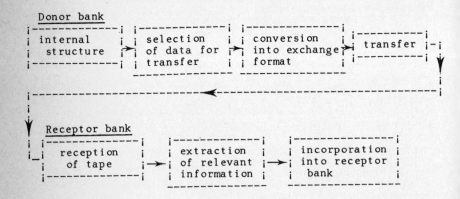

Figure 3.2 Transfer of terminological data via exchange format
(adapted from Rondeau, forthcoming)

An exchange format is based on the principle that the data to be exchanged are transformed by the donor bank into the appropriate exchange format. The receptor bank knows the format of the tape it receives and can then extract all or part of the information according to its needs for incorporation into its own files. Figure 3.2 illustrates this process in simplified form.

3.7.2. Exchange format proposed by ISO/TC 37/WG 4

In 1979, after lengthy discussion, working group 4 of ISO technical committee 37 developed a draft International Standard (ISO/DIS 6156) entitled 'Magnetic Tape Exchange Format for Terminological/Lexicographic Records (MATER)'. This International Standard is designed for information interchange on magnetic tape. The information concerned consists of various monolingual or multilingual terminological or lexicographic data used for this type of exchange. It is also meant to enable users implementing a set of mutually compatible data categories to interchange terminological/lexicographic information with the aid of data processing techniques.

The Standard specifies the requirements for a generalised format, the definition and the layout of terminological/lexicographic data on magnetic tape, as well as the meaning and the layout of the tags associated to each element. It describes an interchange principle between data processing systems but does not aim at defining how or in which form a user's own system is managed.

It should be noted that this standard is proposed only for purely terminological data and not for the documentation or bibliographical references accompanying such records. ISO 2709 specifies a format for the exchange of bibliographical data.

3.8 EXAMPLES OF TERM BANKS

3.8.1 NORMATERM

NORMATERM was set up in the early 1970s by the French national standards organisation AFNOR (Association française de normalisation). It is a prime example of a term bank with an essentially normative attitude to language, and contains only standardised terms or their considered equivalents, to which value judgement labels are attached in cases of synonymy. Its first objective is to list and make available for use the technical terminology contained in French standards and regulations as published in France's Journal officiel and in the standards and recommendations of ISO. It also contains the vocabulary of the International Electrotechnical Commission (IEC) in French and English, which is considered to be of the same reliability as standardised terminology. Though limited in scope, NORMATERM represents therefore a collection of the greatest importance for international cooperation because the terms included are pre-selected for their particular significance in international communication, being widely used with fully agreed definitions by a great number of countries, and the basis for neologisms in many languages. In 1984, the bank held some 150,000 terms and definitions.

NORMATERM provides AFNOR staff with complete, up-to-date information on the terms contained in French and ISO standards which assists its working groups in the elaboration of new and revised standards. Linked with NORIA (AFNOR's documentation system) through the use of the same index file and the same software, the total system provides access to complete documentation on standards terminology. Industry and commerce also use this term bank in order to check on accepted usage, and on the regulations and terminology relating to particular products, processes, etc. in France and abroad.

The AFNOR term bank is able to answer a variety of query types in diverse output formats. In batch mode, it can provide:

1 complete term records, for use especially by terminologists and by AFNOR working groups;

2 monolingual alphabetic indices by keyword, giving: term, generic term, document number, concept number and registration number of concept;

3 bilingual (French-English, English-French) corresponding indices giving: term, synonyms in preferential order, equivalent term plus synonym, document number, concept number and registration number of concept;

4 alphabetic or systematic glossaries by subject area giving: term, definition, hierarchic relations, antonym, associated terms;

5 replies to questions on vocabulary using ISO thesaurus descriptors. This facility would, for example, allow a user to retrieve a term, knowing only its definition.

In addition, microfiches of any part of the data base are available on special request in a variety of formats, with supplements every two months. The NORMATERM index is published in book form every six months and a telephone enquiry service is available. NORMATERM can also be interrogated on-line by its system specialists who deal with user queries. A wide range of search facilities is available, including a field selection facility enabling different term record fields to be examined individually, and string search facilities which ensure exhaustive searches for information on terms whose interrogation form may differ slightly from the data base form. Abbreviations can be the subject of a search as can the various elements of a complex term. Retrieval can take place from French or English, or from a definition using ISO descriptors.

3.8.2 Banque de Terminologie du Québec (BTQ)

In 1974, the terminology centre of the Office de la langue française of the provincial government of Quebec created two initial data bases, Terminoq 1 for terminology and Terminoq 2 for documents containing terminology. By 1980, these had grown to form a bank containing 900,000 term records.

The purpose of the term bank is to serve as a vehicle for the Office de la langue française in its efforts to maintain an effective French language terminology in all areas of Canadian life. It therefore acts as an information service as well as a terminology service and is used both by the Office for its language planning and publicity functions and by the general public for its technical dictionary needs. Over the years of its existence, its function has been changing; whereas in the 1970s it was largely concerned with the distribution of standardised terminology and with implementing the policy of ensuring the survival of the French language in all areas of life in Canada, in the 1980s it has become a dynamic French Canadian dictionary as well as a data base for dictionaries.

The term bank has a wide variety of users including independent translators, private firms, government departments and other public bodies as well as the Office de la langue française itself, which, in 1983, made 40,000 individual enquiries. Of these, 74 per cent were completely successful and a further 11 per cent were partially successful. This response rate was such that the service could be made generally available. In 1984, there were already 160 subscribers, mainly from Quebec, but also from the other provinces of Canada, the USA and Europe. Access to the BTQ is either on-line or by a request for printout in the case of larger queries. A telephone enquiry service is also available. In addition, the term bank publishes glossaries of selected areas of its holdings.

3.8.3 Terminology Bank of Canada (TBC/Termium)

Since Canada is a bilingual country all its federal government business is transacted and recorded in both English and French. The government therefore maintains a very large translation department which is serviced by a terminology section of over one hundred staff. With the development of automation, the existing files of the translation department were converted into machine-readable form and supplemented in the mid-1970s by the addition of the terminology bank of the University of Montreal.

The goals of the Terminology Bank of Canada, 'Termium', are to improve the productivity of translators, to provide reliable terminology in English and French, to standardise the terminology of the acts and regulations of government departments and to enhance the quality of communication in the public services of Canada. It therefore exercises a controlling function over language in the public sector. The majority of its over 2,000 users are translators in the service of the Canadian government. Most of these principal users have direct access to the term bank via a terminal and can receive immediate responses to their queries, on-screen or in computer printout. Average query response time is about five seconds. The bank can also be consulted by telephone or by correspondence. In addition, large masses of data are produced on an indirect basis, in the form of, for example, bilingual glossaries.

Terminological data are stored in three files: a working file, a transit file and a master file. The bank also includes a system for the classification of terminological data, controlled by means of a multi-level thesaurus covering 55 fields. The most recently published figures quote its holdings as more than 1,320,500 terms distributed over 736,000 records.

3.8.4 TEAM

The TEAM (Terminologie Erfassungs- und Auswertungsmethode) term bank was set up in 1967 by the Translation Service of the multinational firm Siemens in Munich. It represents a rationalisation in a large translation and language service in order to increase efficiency and to market the considerable store of multilingual technical vocabulary accumulated by Siemens over many years of translation and technical writing.

TEAM's principal objective is to provide its users with rapid access to all the terminological information they require. Within Siemens, it is used by translators, technical writers, compilers of advertising material, personnel learning a foreign language, and so on. It is increasingly also available to partner companies and independent, external subscribers.

The language services of Siemens hold a number of separate data bases divided into pools, the accumulated holdings of which are given as approximately one million entries, practically all of which are in German with at least one foreign language equivalent. This amounts to a total of some 3 - 4 million terms available for interrogation, although the actual number of individual search terms is probably less than this figure because of the overlap between pools.

The million or so entries in TEAM in French, English, Spanish, Russian, Italian, Portuguese, Dutch and German are mainly derived from the very wide range of subjects in which documentation is required by Siemens with emphasis on electronics and electrical engineering. The vocabulary held by Siemens for its partners and outside users complements the range of terminology developed in-house, being from fields as diverse as economics and sport. Besides its substantial holdings in European languages, TEAM is also developing Arabic terminology and in this connecton collaborates with the Bureau of Arabisation in Cairo.

TEAM can be accessed on- or off-line, and a wide range of types of output is available, in the form of text-oriented lists, alphabetical lists (by subject field, by project, etc.), monolingual indices, word/text concordances, phraseological glossaries and statistical information. Of these available tools, the text-oriented glossaries (i.e. terms and associated information in the order in which they appear in the text to be translated) are particularly popular, as are the alphabetical lists of terms in a specific subject field which help to ensure consistency within a team of translators working on a large project.

In on-line, conversational mode, users have several functions at their disposal, allowing exhaustive searches in the data base. The handling of multi-word terms in particular is organised in such a way that some information on parts of terms at least will be output, if these parts exist in the data base. Starting with at least one subject area code, the following functions are available:

Operations on entry term:

- individual term search;
- by paging through the data base in alphabetical order of the source language, multi-word terms beginning with the required term may be retrieved;
- by marking the entry term as a keyword entry, an automatic display of single and multi-word terms containing this keyword is initiated;
- if a multi-word term is not found in its entirety, then the system automatically asks for equivalents of constituent elements of the term and continues the search.

Operations on strings:

- a powerful string search facility is available, which will search for all terms beginning with, or containing, a certain sequence. This search also yields the number of occurrences of the search string in the data base, and/or the number of occurrences of the string in the target language. String search may also be used as an aid to finding multi-word terms.

Operations on abbreviations:

- abbreviations are treated like terms, and are subject to similar operations.

All on-line operations are provided with flexible parameters to access combinations of individual record fields and to display the information accordingly.

A particularly noteworthy feature of the TEAM system is that it allows on-line translation of texts, by combining with a text processing system to scan a given text and give an interlinear display of translation equivalents for any terms on which it has information.

3.8.5 TERMDOK

The TERMDOK system dates from 1968 when the Swedish Centre of Technical Terminology, Tekniska Nomenclaturcentralen (TNC) established a test terminological file and began to study methods of producing glossaries by means of computerised phototypesetting. The system was developed in order to assist Swedish and other Scandinavian governmental organisations in the introduction of technical and scientific neologisms and in the translation of texts from and into their languages.

The purpose of TERMDOK coincides with that of TNC, which is the first and as yet only European organisation specifically created for the processing and dissemination of multilingual terminology. The need for such a tool in Sweden is that of any highly industrialised and exporting country with what is, in terms of speakers and world distribution, a minor language.

TERMDOK is used by translators, technical writers, terminologists and standardisation specialists. It is used by SIS, the Swedish Standards Institute, to supply material for working groups, and to provide facilities for the control and standardistaion of Swedish terminology. It is used by TNC to prepare glossaries of standardised and non-standardised terms. As a member of NORDTERM, it is used by member terminology states in Scandinavia to help eliminate duplicated work and to assist in terminological coordination generally. It is consulted by SCANNET data-network users and by sponsors and subscribers in Government departments and industry.

TERMDOK is concerned not only with terminological data, but also with lists of addresses and documentary data. The data base is conceptually structured and therefore appears smaller than others without this being a clear indication of its real size. As up to ten languages can be represented on any one record, and many records have all four Scandinavian languages besides English, French, German and Spanish, the indicated holdings of 28,000 terms (in 1978) contain a multiple of that number of search terms. TERMDOK also holds external collections of some 17,500 terms; 30,000 terms from Swedish Standards have also been added.

The new 3RIP system provides for batch output of conceptually organised glossaries with term equivalents and definitions, and of alphabetically ordered vocabularies giving deprecated synonyms. Users working on-line can create their own working file from the data base though some restrictions may operate. They may create their own commands and assign search types or work with pre-defined sets of commands and search types. Infinitely varied output formats are possible in all TNC's languages; hence, they can be tailored to suit the needs of different user groups. TNC also run a telephone reply service, free of charge.

3.8.6 LEXIS

LEXIS was developed by the Bundessprachenamt of the Federal Republic of Germany. Initially, its use was restricted to the Federal German Ministry of Defence for storing the vocabulary required in its translation services. Later, as the functions of the Bundessprachenamt were enlarged to encompass work for other government departments and the teaching of foreign languages, the scope of LEXIS was expanded and its range of users increased.

The primary objective of LEXIS is to assist specialised translators and to promote cooperation, in the form of exchanges of terminologies, of methodological information and of personnel. Its principal users are in-house translators and terminologists. Translation is mainly into German and is highly specialised in a fairly wide range of subjects, and in a wide variety of text types. Translators work primarily with microfiches or printouts of term data, the preferred form of which is the text-oriented term list. Terminologists use LEXIS to provide terminological data for various government departments. Outside users are active in an advisory capacity on standards committees and other language planning activities. LEXIS facilities are also used by documentation/information centres and by language teachers of the Bundessprachenamt.

In 1980, LEXIS had quoted holdings of 1,433,000 German terms of which approximately 62 per cent had equivalents in English, 22 per cent in Russian, 15 per cent in French, and only 1 per cent in other languages (Dutch, Portuguese and Italian). These represent a maximum of 2,866,000 terms available for interrogation. The bank covers some 250 subject fields, including geology, medicine, aeronautics, astronautics, defence, ship building, economics and law. The larger fields have over 10,000 terms in English and German. The number of term records has been growing steadily and between 25,000 and 30,000 new entries are added each year.

The LEXIS system places emphasis on indirect methods of data distribution, in the form of microfiches, full-size or reduced-size printouts, or phototypeset dictionaries. Several kinds of batch output are available, namely, subject field glossaries, various alphabetical listings, and text-oriented glossaries. All translators receive microfiches of the entire content of LEXIS with annual updates.

On-line interrogation is also possible but is primarily at the disposal of terminologists (translators work mainly with various forms of hard copy). Search operations on individual terms, elements of terms and given strings are possible and a paging facility allows browsing in the data base. However, output displays are of limited, fixed format.

3.8.7 EURODICAUTOM

The term bank of the European Communities in Luxembourg and Brussels was officially created in 1973. Its objectives are to control and unify the terminology in the institutions of the EEC and its member states, and to improve the quality of translation, the productivity of translators and the availability of reliable terminological data.

The demand for high quality translations, which are vital in a European Community context where all translations have equal status with original texts, can only be satisfied if translators can rely on common and agreed terminology in all Community languages. Because of the innovatory nature and wide interdisciplinary subject coverage of many of the documents to be translated, existing reference tools proved incomplete and unreliable. So, a new technique of dictionary entry-making and consultation was developed, that of providing phrasal and sentential contexts for the head words, permitting searches not only on head words but on shorter and longer units, and of supplying responses not only of full matches but also of partial matches or words in context.

EURODICAUTOM is used primarily by translators and interpreters working for the CEC; terminals and VDU facilities are also available in the Council of Ministers and in the European Parliament. A number of outside institutions in various EEC member states have direct links with EURODICAUTOM (e.g. the Copenhagen Business School, which has provided Danish terminology). It is also available to the general public via the EURONET-DIANE network.

EURODICAUTOM is informative rather than prescriptive. Nonetheless, the bank's terminologists are very concerned with the quality of the texts from which they collect terms and, in principle, terms are extracted only from original texts. To assist with quality control, the bank has introduced a 'reliability rating' on a scale of 0 to 5, which indicates the reliability of the terminological information in terms of the presence or absence of authoritative reference sources. The rating 0 is assigned to information for which no source can be given, and the rating 5 to information from standards or documents considered equivalent.

The data provided by the main supplier, the Terminology Bureau of Luxembourg, are terms in context, or even phraseological units. The job of the EURODICAUTOM terminologist is to locate equivalent terms in their own contexts, preferably in all the languages in use in the bank. The bank also contains differently structured terminological data from other sources, e.g. the term bank of the University of Montreal and the BTQ. The total number of term records is approximately 310,000, in addition to which a large sub-bank of some 85,000 abbreviations has recently been developed.

Several modes of consultation and types of output are possible. For example, in batch mode, a user can specify the subject code and the languages in which an answer is required and receive a reponse within 24 hours on a central line printer. The combination of direct on-line consultation and immediate printout is also available for translators. In conversational mode, users have a wide variety of facilities at their disposal.

3.8.8 Other term banks and ongoing projects

In addition to the major term banks we have described, there is a number of other smaller banks which deserve to be mentioned. These include DANTERM developed at the Copenhagen School of Economics and Business Administration, CEZEAU3 at the Centre Universitaire des Sciences et Techniques of the University of Clermont-Ferrand, NoTe, a Norwegian term bank set up in 1979, and the term bank of the West German firm Ruhrgas AG.

The impetus to create new term banks is constantly growing. At UMIST in Manchester, research is currently under way towards the establishment of a British term bank. Similarly, the ongoing HISPANOTERM project has the goal of establishing a national term bank for Spain.

3.9 FURTHER READING

(Unlike other chapters of this book, the references for further reading on term banks are not structured by section. Instead, we have divided the further reading for Chapter 3 into general material on terminology and term banks, detailed literature on individual term banks, comparative surveys of banks, and items which focus on specific topics in term bank research.)

63

General
AFTERM (1976, 1978), Bakulina (1979), CEC (1977), Felber et al. (1979) and Snell (1983) are useful collections of articles covering various aspects of terminology and term banks. For an introduction to terminology see Rondeau (1981), the English translation of which is due to be published shortly.

Individual term banks
NORMATERM (and the terminological activities of AFNOR): AFNOR (1973, 1975), de Bessé (1976, 1979), Clerc and Laurent (1976), Clerc (1980), Laurent (1976, 1977), Levy (1978b).

BTQ: Fortin (1974), Fortin and Lebel-Harou (1976).

TBC: Dubuc (1972, 1975), Hortzwath (1975) and Terminology and Documentation Directorate (1977). Paré (1974) discusses the bank at the University of Montreal.

TEAM: Brinkmann (1975, 1979), Brunold (1976), de Bessé (1978), Schulz and Goricke (1977). Its cooperative work with the German standards institute DIN is discussed in Brinkmann (1979).

TERMDOK: Sundstrom's article (1978a) gives an introduction; a more detailed treatment is found in Sundstrom (1978b). Information on TERMDOK also appears regularly in the Termdok Bulletin (Sundstrom ed.) For information on the new 3RIP system see TNC (1980).

LEXIS: Berner (1976), Hoffmann (1978). For an account in English see Krollmann (1978).

EURODICAUTOM: Goetschalckx (1977), Sager (1979). Most references are in French, notably, François (1976), Reichling (1976, 1978), Levy (1978a), Vollmer (1979).

Danterm: DANTERM (1979), and paper by Frandsen and Nistrup (1979).

NoTe: Hjulstad (1984)

The British Term Bank Project: McNaught (1981), Sager and McNaught (1981a, 1981b, 1981c), Sager and Price (1983).

HISPANOTERM: INFOTERM (1980).

Comparative surveys
Sager and McNaught (1981b) is a selective survey of European term banks; Hvalkof (1982) is also selective, but includes BTQ and TBC. The most up-to-date, detailed information on term banks is provided in the comprehensive study by de Bessé and Mosler (1985).

Specific topics
Aspects of data exchange between term banks are examined in McNaught and Nkwenti Azeh (1983).

4   Machine translation

The use of the computer to translate texts from one language to another is perhaps the most obvious application in the field of multilingual information processing. Although machine translation (MT) is no longer in its infancy (the first proposal for the use of computers to do translation actually predates the appearance of the first modern computer by about a year), it comes as a surprise to many people to learn that we are still far from the day when machines will be able to translate texts with the same fluency and accuracy as human translators.

MT has had a chequered history, caused not least by the naive view that translation is simply a question of looking words up in a dictionary and writing down the result, and hence a straightforward, routine task which is eminently suitable for entrusting to a computer. The 'dark age' of machine translation, from the mid 1960s to the mid 1970s, was largely brought on by the disappointing results of attempts to put this unsophisticated approach into practice. The 'renaissance' of MT which began in the late 1970's, and which shows every sign of continuing, owes its inception to the real need to supplement the inadequate translation resources of companies and institutions to meet the ever-increasing demands of an information-hungry technological society, and owes its continuance to a much more pragmatic acceptance of the limited abilities of computers in the area of translation. Moreover, the progress which has been made in the last 20 years towards a better understanding of the nature of language and translation leads workers in MT today to make much more modest, but at the same time more responsible claims about what the computer can contribute to easing the problems of information dissemination in a multilingual world.

In this chapter we shall first look briefly at the early history of MT, to see how and why it failed so dramatically and inevitably, followed by an overview of some of the developments of the last ten years (4.1). We then look at various ways in which computers are now being used to assist the translation process without necessarily performing unaided the entire activity from input of a source language text to delivery of the finished product (4.2).

Building on this background material, we shall consider some of the basic theoretical and design principles in modern MT thinking (4.3); this combines together ideas and insights from the major contributing fields of linguistics and computer science, which are also surveyed (4.4). The chapter concludes by considering how MT research and output is (or should be) evaluated (4.5), and with a little crystal ball gazing into the probable future directions which MT might take (4.6).

4.1 BACKGROUND

Most commentators trace the history of MT back to the years following
the end of the Second World War, when the attentions of those involved
in wartime computer-assisted code breaking were turned to the more
challenging task of translation proper. The famous memorandum sent by
Warren Weaver to 200 of his colleagues in 1949 is felt to mark the
birth of MT research, and its content clearly reflects the experience
in cryptanalysis of its author:

> When I look at an article in Russian, I say: 'This is really
> written in English, but it has been coded in some strange
> symbols. I will now proceed to decode.' (letter from Weaver
> to Norbert Wiener of MIT (4 March 1947), quoted in Weaver,
> 1949, p.18.)

Thus was launched in the early 1950s a programme of intense activity
in the USA with government aid of around $20m being granted to some 20
institutions over the period 1954-1964. The principal aim of this
work, in keeping with the political mood of the time, was Russian-
English translation, with the government sponsors seeking an efficient
means of keeping its military and scientific community informed of
Soviet activity on various fronts.

But the honeymoon came to a rapid end when in 1964 the US National
Academy of Sciences sponsored an investigation into MT research, and
in 1966 the Automated Language Processing Advisory Committee (ALPAC)
published its findings in a now notorious report. MT was found to be
slower, more expensive and less reliable than human translation, and
the report's conclusions that

> ...we do not have useful machine translation. Furthermore,
> there is no immediate or predictable prospect of useful
> machine translation (ALPAC, 1966, p.32)

effectively sounded the death knell for MT research in the USA. In
fact, ALPAC's findings were not all bad, since the report recommended
resources be diverted towards the more practical areas of automated
information processing, including machine dictionaries, information
retrieval, automatic character recognition and even machine aided
translation. The ALPAC report itself was attacked, notably by
Pankowicz (1967), who challenged the report for inferior analytical
work resulting in factual inaccuracies, its hostile and vindictive
attitude, its use of obsolete and invalid facts and figures,
distortion of quality, speed and cost estimates in favour of human
translation and concealment of data reflecting credit on MT.

But as far as MT proper was concerned, the ALPAC report signalled
the cessation of all government funding, and the effective winding up
of almost all work on the subject, at least in the USA.

The reasons for this disaster are, in retrospect, not hard to find.
Over-optimism as a result of early promising results was the main

problem, and was spotted by some even before ALPAC, witness
Oettinger's comment in 1963:

> The notion of ... fully automatic high quality mechanical
> translation, planted by overzealous propagandists for
> automatic translation ... and nurtured by the wishful
> thinking of potential users, blossomed like a vigorous weed.
> (Oettinger, 1963, p.18)

The problem with the early 'first generation' MT systems (see below)
on which ALPAC based its conclusions was their basically naive
approach to translation. Any person with the least training in a
foreign language should have been able to predict the limitations of a
system based essentially on word-for-word translation with a small
degree of local word-order reorganisation. Yet this was the typical
arrangement of these early systems, organised around very large
dictionaries, but with little or no underlying linguistic theory. It
is clear how this approach produced initially promising results, but
how, after the initial progress, the only improvements possible were
restricted to ad hoc tinkering with local linguistic context and
massive enlargement of dictionaries to cover one new special case
after another.

MT research did not cease entirely following the ALPAC report. Even
in the USA private funding enabled work based on the Georgetown
University systems to continue in the form of SYSTRAN, a system still
in use in a variety of establishments. Outside the USA, notable MT
research centres were in Montreal and Grenoble. The TAUM group
(Traduction Automatique `a l'Université de Montréal) were developing
the METEO system, funded by the Canadian government, to translate
weather bulletins from English into French, while in Grenoble at CETA
(Centre d'Etudes pour la Traduction Automatique) work on Russian-
French MT, begun in 1961, continued. At both these centres, research
represented a significant departure from the model of the 'first
generation' systems, with approaches that were both computationally
and linguistically more sophisticated. Both fields had quite
independently undergone something of a revolution, which these MT
centres were to benefit from. Chomsky had shown that linguistics
could be profitably formalised, while improved techniques were also
being adopted from computer science: METEO was implemented using Alain
Colmerauer's 'Q-systems', while the CETA approach was based on the
production systems approach originally developed for modelling
cognitive processes. Both these approaches are discussed further
below.

We should not ignore in this historical overview other contemporary
systems. In the early 1970s significant MT systems were being
developed at Saarbrücken in Germany (SUSY: initially German-French,
later other target languages) and at the Chinese University of Hong
Kong (CULT: translating the Chinese journal Acta Mathematica Sinica
into English). Information from the Soviet Union was then, as now,
difficult to verify, but certainly some research was taking place.
Despite ALPAC, other political considerations led to work on an
English-Vietnamese translation system, LOGOS, funded by the US Air
Force. Surveys of MT around this time reflected the resurgent

interest in MT, but were probably misleading as to the number of MT systems in existence at the time, since they tended not to differentiate between MT interest groups and locations where systems were running and producing output.

By the late 1970s, as the last statement suggests, MT had become a more respectable topic, and interested parties were taking a more theoretical rather than engineering approach, deliberating in greater depth on what MT involved. Yehoshua Bar-Hillel's pronouncement in 1960 that fully automatic high-quality machine translation (FAHQ-MT) was unattainable had paved the way for the ALPAC body-blow, but the same person was able, eleven years later, to express a new awareness of the problems:

> It seems, then, that we have come full circle in MT research and are now approximately back where we started some nineteen years ago.... It is quite clear that the detour has enormously helped to clarify the issue, has dispersed any utopian hopes so that we are now in a much better position to attack this problem afresh. (Bar-Hillel, 1971, p.75)

The CETA and METEO systems had already recognised the need to aim for an analysis of the source text that went beyond the surface level. Victor Yngve, as early as 1967, went further in suggesting that

> Work in MT has come up against what we will call the semantic barrier. Even when we have programs which can give grammatical analyses of the incoming sentences, we still cannot make adequate translations because of the large amount of remaining ambiguity. We have come face to face with the realization that we will only have adequate machine translations when the machine can 'understand' what it is translating and this will be a very difficult task indeed. (Yngve, 1967, p.500)

Although the question of the necessity to understand in order to translate is highly debatable - and note Yngve's cautious use of quotes around the key word - an important distinction was recognised between linguistic knowledge, contextual knowledge, and real-world knowledge. These are issues to which we shall return, but they are historically significant in that they paved the way for the further approach - hailed by some as the 'third generation', but still not significantly incorporated into any working system - of meaning-based MT. Prototype systems along these lines were developed at Stanford University, and more recently at Yale.

This brings us to the present, and we can conclude this historical survey with a view of MT in the early 1980s. Of most significance is the massive surge of interest in the subject, as witnessed by several conferences and special issues of journals. Several machine-aided translation systems are available commercially (see below), while the renewed confidence in MT is reflected by the commitment of the European Commission to the Eurotra project, and the acceptance of MT as an important part of the Japanese 'fifth-generation' computer scheme. The renamed Grenoble team GETA (Groupe d'Etudes pour la Traduction Automatique) continues to be funded by the French government, while in Austin, Texas, the LRC group (Linguistic Research Center) has developed in a very short time a highly successful German-English system, METAL, thanks to the funding by the industrial sponsor Siemens, based in Munich. SYSTRAN, now based in La Jolla, California, and translating several language pairs, continues to be sold to and/or developed by various centres, including Rank-Xerox, General Motors, Wang, the European Commission, the US Air Force, and several others. Smaller, more experimental projects, are funded by Philips in Eindhoven (Dutch-English), by the Pan American Health Organisation in Washington (Spanish-English), and by ICL and UMIST in Manchester (English-Japanese). Even at the time of writing, there are no doubt other equally worthy projects underway, and, given the new rate of development of this 'born-again' science, we can admit that details given here will rapidly become out of date.

4.2 MODES AND USES

The original idea of MT, which still persists even today in some quarters, was of a fully automatic process where a computer is given a text in one language and produces as output a finished version of the same text in another. As we have already seen, it became apparent very early on that the attainment of such an optimistic goal was not even obviously feasible.

The current attitude among MT workers is very different and their aims are now much more realistic. There are now essentially two, not necessarily incompatible, schools of thought on the practical applications of MT in the foreseeable future. One view, which derives more or less directly from the early MT tradition, is that MT can be used to produce 'pre-translations', to be revised subsequently by skilled translators acting as 'post-editors'; the texts to be translated may also be 'pre-edited' by skilled operators to make them more suitable for machine consumption (CULT is a good example of this). The second position is that machines are very good and efficient at doing some things, like looking up target language equivalents of technical terms, storing and retrieving text, and some limited forms of linguistic analysis (parsing, see section 1.5); humans are good at other things, such as disambiguating pronoun references, capturing nuances of style or choosing the 'right' translation equivalent of a word when a wide choice is available. In this view, a desirable aim is to partition the task of translation so that humans and computers each do the things that they can do best, and in doing so each helps the other to produce a high quality result in an efficient way.

The first position is often characterised as 'Human assisted machine translation' (HAMT), in contrast to the second, which is described as 'Machine aided human translation' (MAHT). Although these labels are sufficently similar to be easily confused, and also suggest a more clearcut division of relative responsibilities than is actually the case, they are nevertheless quite widely used.

4.2.1 Machine aided human translation (MAHT)

Any craftsman relies on good tools to do a job well, and the translator is no exception. The typical tools of a translator are:

1 those that are common to anyone concerned with the production of text, such as technical reference works, monolingual dictionaries, style guides and typewriters;

2 those which are peculiar to the task of translation, notably bilingual dictionaries and bilingual or multilingual specialised terminologies.

As the cost of computing power decreases and computers are coming to be more and more widely accepted as standard office equipment, so we are led to ask to what extent computerisation is being used to supplement or even replace the translator's traditional toolkit.

We have already seen, in the last chapter, how much of an impact the computer has already had on the world of lexicography, not only in the preparation of dictionaries and terminologies for publication, but in the actual day-to-day activity of a typical translation department. In this section, we review briefly the consequences of the trend towards automation of general office functions, and then look at recent and imminent attempts to extend and specialise general facilities for text processing into a purpose-built environment designed to assist translators.

4.2.1.1 Text processing

The most obvious case of the impact of computers on the world of text preparation and production is the humble word processor, and its more sophisticated cousin the electronic typesetter. A direct descendant of the typewriter, the word processor has by now almost completely replaced its ancestor in offices. In the simplest case, the only real difference between the two is that documents which once had to be drafted and redrafted on the typewriter, going through several generations of revisions requiring retyping each time, can now, with a word processor, be typed directly on to the screen, revised on the screen, reformatted and restructured on the screen, printed off when judged to be ready for distribution, and even saved for future use.

This is the simplest case. Today's word processors already have many more sophisticated features which can contribute to removing effort from producing output of professional quality. There are facilities for re-using the same text many times, with small modifications made automatically to each version, as, for example in printing off standard circulars with each copy individually named and addressed. All but the cheapest word processors now contain some kind of 'spelling correction', usually in the form of a standard dictionary against which each word of the document is compared; any word which is not found in the dictionary is highlighted on the screen and the author is given various options: to change the word in the text, leave it as it is, add a new word to the dictionary, and so on.

In more sophisticated systems, of which IBM's EPISTLE is a good example, processing of the text extends to what is called 'style checking'. Rather than simply looking up words in a dictionary, these systems are able to check that, to a certain extent, the words have been put together correctly. In other words, they check not just spelling, but also syntax. The kind of errors that such systems can spot quite easily are typical careless errors such as failure to make verbs agree with their subject (e.g. Your statement of deficiencies have not been completed – should be has), wrong use of pronouns (e.g. The contract was written by Joe Smith and I – should be me), noun-modifier disagreement (e.g. Several of the misplaced memo were found in the files – should be memoes), incorrect verb forms (e.g. The manuscript was wrote by Tom Brown – should be written), and non-parallel structures (e.g. We will accept funds, send receipts, and crediting accounts – should be credit). Wrong usage of discontinuous structures like either...or, both...and, rather...than, can also be corrected. Finally, typical mistyping mistakes like duplicating words such as articles, prepositions and so on can often be spotted, as can certain omissions. In each case, the method used is to perform a syntactic parse of the text, and to indicate places in the text where this parse fails. Obviously the range of errors that can be spotted in this way depends on the sophistication of the grammar used to guide the parser.

Further facilities take advantage of the fact that most word processors are built using general purpose microprocessors, so that the machine can be used equally well as an electronic filing system, storing not only master copies of previous documents for consultation or re-use but also useful reference information like catalogues, price lists, formulae, diagrams ... the list is endless. Moreover, most modern word processors allow the screen to be divided up into a number of smaller screens, usually called 'windows', with each window displaying independently different kinds of information. Thus, one window can be used to prepare text, while another displays part numbers and prices, a third acts as a scratch-pad on which the writer jots down notes which may be useful later, and so on.

4.2.1.2 The 'translator's workbench'

Here already there is a formidable array of useful facilities for translators, apart from the convenience afforded by using a word processor in the first place. For example, one window on the screen can be used to display the text to be translated while the translation is being prepared in the second. Parallel scrolling is obviously desirable too: standard word processors allow the user to access rapidly different sections of a text; in a translation environment, this scrolling feature must operate simultaneously on both texts. A third window can be reserved for looking up words in an electronic dictionary or text-oriented glossary, perhaps prepared on another machine and stored on a floppy disk. What is more, the cost of word processing is such that facilities like these are already, or soon will be, within the reach of any professional.

Incorporation of modern hardware tools like touch-sensitive screens, light pens, or 'mice' could make the design of a translator-friendly word processor an exciting prospect. Imagine for example a facility where the translator can indicate a word in the source text using one of these devices, and immediately a window opens up, in a suitable area of the screen, showing the dictionary information associated with this word.

Given that all these things are possible, an obvious question is whether it is also possible to integrate them together to produce a single, specialised environment for translators, in which as many as possible of the useful functions like dictionary look-up are actually done automatically. The answer is yes, and systems now exist which produce, in a word processor environment, a draft translation which the human translator can then work on to produce a polished version. We shall discuss the availability and usefulness of such systems below, but let us first see how, typically, such systems work.

We shall assume that the text to be translated has already been entered, whether typed in in the normal manner or by some automatic means (an 'optical character recognition' type face exists, and can be 'read' using appropriate hardware and software). The first phase is usually one of dictionary look-up coupled with morphological analysis (see section 1.2). Here, the source text is scanned and each word looked up in the system's dictionary. Grammatical words are usually bypassed at this stage, and the 'target text' produced corresponds to the source text but with 'lexical' words replaced by their target-language equivalents. Often, there is a choice of possible translations for a given source word, and the translator will be asked to choose from a selection. Alternatively, the system may make its own choice, either on the basis of a text-type or subject-matter code, or by asking the user to distinguish between two likely readings, e.g. faced with translating room into French, the system may ask if this is the general concept 'spaciousness' (place), or part of a house (pièce), and if the latter, whether large (salle) or small (chambre) and so on. If a word is not in the dictionary, the user will be asked to provide the correct translation, and may even be invited to enter a sequence of dictionary up dating, so that the new word is stored for subsequent recognition.

Once this lexical phase is complete, the system will, depending on its sophistication, attempt to produce a draft translation. In existing systems, this usually involves a fairly rudimentary translation, comparable in quality to that of early full MT systems. This generally means adhering fairly rigidly to the structure of the original text, though in existing systems at least low-level elements like noun phrases are often handled quite well. Thorny problems such as recognising pronoun antecedents, and disambiguating structural ambiguities (e.g. prepositional phrase attachment) are usually left to the human translator, though in fact it sometimes happens that a literal translation turns out to be acceptable.

The attraction of these systems is that their designers recognise and work within the limits of what can be achieved in reasonable processing time: even half a minute is a long time for a user to sit in front of a blank screen waiting for output, and the underlying design criterion is that the human has ultimate control over the quality of the translation. In the worst case, the user can abandon the machine's effort for a given portion of text and tackle it from scratch. In the best case, the machine may produce a wholly acceptable translation.

Such systems are now produced and marketed commercially by firms such as Weidner, ALPS and LOGOS, all based in the USA, but with outlets in Europe. Unfortunately, commercial MAHT systems at present are not available independent of their associated hardware in the form of large mainframe computers, and this tends to put them beyond the means of independent translators, or even small firms. At Brigham Young University in Utah, however, Alan Melby is conducting research work to develop a micro-based MAHT system, the name of which we have borrowed for the title of this section. But the larger commercial systems are indeed bought and used by larger companies, whose translation needs justify the outlay. A client with a sufficiently large daily turnover of translations might see investment in a MAHT system as a viable alternative to sending translations out to agencies and freelancers. The short turn-around time is particularly attractive. But the main reason for the popularity of such systems for certain users is their very specific translation needs. MAHT systems are not currently well-suited for production of higher quality translations of literary, legal or discursive texts. They do however produce reasonable quality translations of technical texts and, even largely unedited, output is often usable when the requirement is general interest in approximate content (translators call this 'gist'), for example to see whether it is worthwhile having a text translated 'properly'. In scientific, industrial and commercial communities where foreign-language skills are not always to the forefront, MAHT systems play an obvious role, especially where texts may be of a style or content which makes them low in job-satisfaction for the translator: agendas of meetings or lists of customers' orders are typical examples. While no one would wish to see MT research restricted to this domain, MAHT has a rightful place in the field as a whole.

4.2.2 Human assisted machine translation (HAMT)

Whereas in the previous section we discussed MAHT systems of varying degrees of sophistication, we wish to discuss in this section the ways in which humans generally intervene in 'MT proper'.

This intervention by humans in the MT process takes two principal forms: before and/or after the machine performs its task ('pre-' and 'post-editing'), or during the machine's processing ('interaction').

4.2.2.1 Pre- and post-editing

Currently, there is no significant MT system which produces consistently usable output without a stage of pre- or post-editing.

Pre-editing involves some degree of text preparation before submission to the machine. This may take the form, in the simplest case, of clarifying textual features such as paragraph or sentence boundaries, indicating portions of the text which are not to be translated (e.g. formulae), or distinguishing headings from running text, where different translation strategies might be implied.

More frequently, however, pre-editing involves a more significant preliminary manipulation of the text, so that foreseeable translation difficulties can be obviated. One typical and obvious practice is to distinguish proper names via some convention which will be recognised by the system as a signal not to attempt a translation. A famous example of what can happen if proper names are not correctly recognised occurred when a text containing the name Georges van Slype was translated into French: in the output this appeared as Georges camion anglaise Slype.

Pre-editing can also take the form of explicitly indicating multiword compounds as single lexical units (e.g. by replacing the intervening spaces by underlines or hyphens: Empire-State-Building), or resolving lexical ambiguities (e.g. Schloss1 'castle' vs Schloss2 'lock'). For an alternative treatment of such problems within the linguistic framework of the system, see below.

Finally, in some systems (e.g. CULT, TITUS), pre-editing may effectively replace a large amount of the task of source text analysis, so that the text eventually submitted to the machine barely resembles natural language at all, but is 'pre-coded' for more or less direct translation.

Of course, the main aim of pre-editing is to ensure a higher quality of translation, and/or to render the mechanised part of the general task more efficient and reliable. There is an inevitable trade-off between the amount of pre-editing required and the sophistication of the system, though it is generally recognised that there is a limit to pre-editing (perhaps corresponding to the point at which it would have been more efficient to have the text translated by a human) beyond which the machine's role can no longer be described as MT as such.

Post-editing consists of taking the output and making whatever corrections are necessary. As such it does not differ significantly, in theory, from the work of editing translations made by human beings, and the amount of editing will depend not only on the quality of the output, but also on the desired quality of the end product. It is interesting to note the extent to which so-called 'raw' output from some MT systems is usable without any post-editing. Sometimes, the end user wants a rough idea of the content of a text so as to decide whether it is worth translating 'properly'. Alternatively, an end user with a little knowledge of the source language might find the raw output, even with some quirks of more or less literal translation, sufficient for his or her particular needs.

One notable feature of MT systems in which the only human intervention is before or after the machine has performed its function is that such systems can, and normally do, run in 'batch' mode. This means that the processing can take place at a time that is most convenient for the general community which has access to the computer: typically such an MT system will not be implemented on a 'dedicated' machine, but will be just one of a number of packages installed on a large general-purpose computer. One can therefore imagine a situation where a translation 'job' is submitted to the computer, the output to be collected later. If it is a big job, an overnight run might be most appropriate. This scenario has one important consequence for the design of such a system, which is that whatever happens, some output must be produced: the system cannot be allowed to 'get stuck' on, say, the first sentence, but should have some way of continuing with the rest of the text, leaving the problem sentence to the post-editors. This feature of MT systems will be discussed in more detail in section 4.4.2.5.

4.2.2.2 Interactive MT

In an alternative approach to the one described above, there is the possibility, during processing, for the system to interact with a human 'operator' whenever it comes across a problem that it cannot resolve alone. This possibility of interaction implies an entirely different approach to MT, and is one which seems to hold a certain amount of promise. At the time of writing, no such system exists in anything more than prototype form, and this is at least one area for MT research of the near future.

We should contrast here the kind of interaction we have in mind with the interaction found in MAHT systems: in MAHT, as we have seen, interaction takes the form of dictionary update for unknown words, this being performed once only for the entire text and before the system begins its translation. Thereafter, there is no further interaction until the system has completed its processing to the best of its ability, at which point it hands control back to the person for substantial post-editing. In interactive MT on the other hand, what is envisaged is an ongoing dialogue between the system and the operator, during which the system will not only update its lexicon, but will seek to have competing analyses disambiguated, and even to make motivated predictions (e.g. about word-classes of unknown words based on morphology or syntax), which the operator will confirm or correct. This approach has already proved successful in some small general language processing systems (e.g. MIND, PTOSYS), and its extension to MT is seen as an exciting area for exploration. In one current research project for example (the UMIST/ICL English-Japanese system mentioned above), the approach is being used to build a translation system for use by a monolingual operator having no knowledge of the target language.

4.3 DESIGN PRINCIPLES

In this section we wish to consider a number of basic principles underlying the general design of an MT system. These are principles that have evolved over the years, but are now largely felt to be essential notions, and as such tend to be restated in many overviews of MT. Where appropriate, we shall direct the reader to the best detailed discussions, since here we can only give a flavour of the fundamental issues.

4.3.1 Transfer vs. interlingua

The first and perhaps most obvious of these is the dichotomy in MT between so-called 'transfer'-based systems, and those which use an 'interlingua'. Discounting the approach found in first generation systems where, as described above, translation was essentially word-for-word with some local word-order reorganisation, it is fair to say that all MT systems involve in some sense an analysis of the source text, and some kind of process of generation of the target text. What happens in between these two phases depends on the transfer-interlingua distinction.

A transfer-based system includes a stage of processing in which the results of source-text analysis – typically some kind of non-linear representation of the source text – is converted into a corresponding representation for the target text, this acting as input to the generation phase. In an interlingua-based system on the other hand, the representation aimed at in the analysis phase serves in itself as input to generation: this representation, usually termed an 'interlingua', is essentially independent of both source and target languages. The distinction between the two types of system is quite nicely illustrated by the now well-known 'triangle' diagram (Figure 4.1). The diagram suggests that the deeper the analysis of the source text, the less complex is the mapping from source-language-based representation to target (the transfer) with, at the top, the interlingua or pivot representation, with no transfer as such at all.

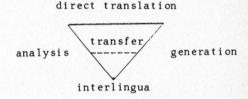

Figure 4.1 Three types of translation system

The main apparent disadvantage with the transfer approach is that as languages are added to the system, the number of transfer modules needed increases exponentially: for n languages, $n(n-1)$ transfer modules are required. This difference is brought out when one compares how the addition of a fourth language involves only an extra analysis and generation module for the interlingual system, but requires an additional eight modules (one analysis, one generation and six transfer) in the transfer model.

The disadvantages of an interlingua-based system are rather more subtle, and result from the practical difficulty of actually defining a language-free interlingual representation. The development of an interlingua for various purposes (not only translation) has been the subject of philosophical debate for some years, and proposals for MT have included the use of formalised natural language, artificial languages, like Esperanto, or various symbolic representations, whether linear or otherwise. Most of these approaches are problematic, however, and this difficulty arises from two sources: lexical and syntactic. Indeed, most of the work on interlinguas has centred on the representation of the lexical content of texts. Although the notion of 'terminological equivalence' (see Chapter 3) is helpful as far as technical vocabulary is concerned, there remains a

large area of the lexicon, including most verbs for example, which
does not form part of the domain of technical terminology for any
subject, and this field is often called 'general-purpose vocabulary'.

Much more problematic for the interlingual approach, however, is the
representation of syntactic structures. A large proportion of
syntactic structures, even when reduced to 'canonical form' (i.e. with
distinctions such as active vs. passive neutralised) remain too
language-specific to act as an interlingual representation, even
between closely related languages. Consider, for example, the number
of verbs which in one language take a prepositional object which in
another language is realised as a direct object (e.g. pay for a meal
- payer un repas). Various 'meaning representations' suggested seem
to be too deep and to involve too much effort in analysis for the
purposes of translation. One possible solution to this problem is to
define an interlingua that is specifically geared towards the
languages in the system, and takes advantage of any accidental
similarities in the structure of the languages concerned, while
attempting to neutralise differences. While this may appear
promising, for example for a large subset of the European languages,
very little success in this direction has so far been achieved. In
particular, there is the difficulty that adding a new language to the
system might involve completely redefining the interlingua, and as a
consequence, rewriting all the analysis and generation modules.
Furthermore, this approach is apparently quite out of the question
with pairs of highly dissimilar languages.

By and large, then, the transfer approach tends to be favoured these
days. Typically, analysis of the source text without taking account
of the target language is pursued up to some predetermined point
(which may be defined more or less arbitrarily as a function of the
relative efficiency of larger or smaller analysis, transfer and
generation modules), at which point strictly language pair-specific
manipulations are performed until a representation is reached from
which the target text can be generated, correspondingly without
acknowledging the original source language. This approach is
particularly inviting in a multilingual system, where the same
strictly monolingual analysis and generation phases can, in principle,
be used for each and every language pair.

It should be noted that in a system that in any case treats only one
language pair, the distinction between transfer and interlingua is
minimised almost to the point of non-existence: in this situation it
would clearly be senseless to ignore any accidental similarities
between the source and target languages, and to the question of where
analysis ceases and transfer begins, or whether indeed there is a
transfer stage, becomes more or less moot.

4.3.2 Separation of algorithms and linguistic data

The second major principle underlying the design of an MT system is
that of separating the essentially computational task of designing and
implementing a computer program, and the essentially linguistic task
of defining a strategy for translating between languages. Early MT
systems combined these two tasks in 'translation programs', whereas
nowadays it is generally recognised that it is desirable to

differentiate between the two sides of the problem.

The disadvantages in the earlier combined approach are fairly clear: first and foremost, it meant that anybody wishing to work on an MT system - either as a designer, implementer, or even anything more than a most passive user - had to have both computer science and linguistics training: a prerequisite for being able to contribute to the development of the system would be knowledge of and skill in using a particular programming language. Typically, in fact, MT pioneers were principally computer scientists, and their linguistic naivety was one of the factors contributing to the failure of first generation MT. Any 'linguistic theory' that was present would in any case be inextricably bound up with the program, and therefore usually quite difficult to recognise.

The second disadvantage is that it is difficult, when the translation process somehow goes wrong, to determine and distinguish whether this is due to a programming error, or a weakness in the linguistic approach.

Finally, in this kind of set-up, the side-effects of apparently quite innocent modifications can sometimes be appallingly far-reaching, and quite difficult to trace.

Although this principle has only relatively recently become an issue in MT, the separation of the definition of a problem and the definition of an algorithmic solution to it has been standard practice for a long time in other areas of knowledge-based programming (cf. the literature on production systems referred to in 4.7).

The possible responses to this principle are discussed in more detail in section 4.4.2, but it is worth noting that at least two of the more successful MT systems in recent years have eschewed this principle, probably because in this way both the time spent developing the system and, to a certain extent, actual run-time efficiency are favourable. SYSTRAN is coded entirely in Fortran, and although the programs are fairly extensively documented, linguists working on the systems must either become familiar with that programming language, or work through the intermediary of a programmer. One result of this approach is that after a long period of extensive development, it now seems that a threshold of performance has been reached which cannot be significantly improved without substantially redesigning the system. In the case of METAL, the separation principle was at least acknowledged in the choice of Lisp as programming language for the greater part of the system: this language has the advantage of having been specifically designed for complex non-numerical computations (see 1.4), and had already been used with some success in a number of different though smaller natural language-oriented programming tasks.

4.3.3 Modularity

Coming hand in hand with the principle of separation as an import from computer science is the principle that the problem of MT is best tackled by breaking it down into a series of steps or modules. This is true of any complex computational task, and the principle of dividing a large task into smaller more or less independent sub-tasks which communicate by means of a strictly defined interface protocol is well documented in computer science.

We have already seen the gross division between analysis and generation (with or without transfer), but there is much scope for further subdivision of tasks. Typical further modularisations might for example separate out (in analysis) dictionary look-up, morphological analysis, immediate constituent recognition, homograph disambiguation, anaphor resolution, (in transfer) lexical substitution, syntactic rearrangement, (and in generation) morphological assignment, string generation, though of course various systems differ in their subdivision of the overall task.

Notice that separation and modularity are not the same thing: both SYSTRAN and METAL, which have no separation as discussed above, are nevertheless highly modular in their approaches. On the other hand, the modular approach may well be reflected in the manner in which the separation is achieved, as in the case with GETA where, as we shall see in more detail in section 4.4.2.4, different modules have associated with them more or less specifically tailored software tools.

Notice too that it is not only elegance that is provided by the modular approach. With the process broken down into strictly defined sub-tasks with corresponding input and output definitions, it is much easier to pinpoint errors and weaknesses by inspecting the partial results of the translation process at specific points of interest. By the same token it is easier to get into the system and make repairs, and unexpected side-effects are minimised and restricted to within the given module. As mentioned above, the modular approach also requires a strictly defined interface protocol, by which is meant the way in which the results of one module are passed to the next. This requirement has lead to a number of interesting developments on the question of representation of partially processed texts, and of the suitability of various data structures for MT (see 4.4.2.3).

4.3.4 Multilingualism

We should briefly return to the question of multilingualism, introduced in the transfer-interlingua debate above. An important design decision is whether the proposed MT system should treat only one language pair; do this in the first instance but with the addition of further languages envisaged; or be multilingual from the outset. Clearly, the difference between the second and third choices is essentially practical, whereas the bilingual vs. multilingual distinction has serious consequences. It was suggested above that in a strictly bilingual system it would make sense to do only as much analysis of the source language as is necessary to enable the target language translation to be correctly generated, thus taking full advantage of any accidental similarities between the two languages. But it should be recognised that this approach more or less precludes the later additions of other languages, since the greater part of a source-language analysis effected within the perspective of a given target language is most likely to be of little or no use for the new language; and the same goes for the generation procedures.

The decision to build a (potentially) multilingual system involves numerous other interesting considerations, not least of which is the transfer vs. interlingua question discussed above. But it also has implications for the design of the interface protocols mentioned in the modularity discussion: should analysis aim at the deepest commonly appropriate representations or should there be a shallower break-off point for pairs of more closely related languages? The linguistic work involved in reconciling three or more languages is considerably more significant than the straightforward contrastive analysis involved with pairs of languages.

4.4 THE CONTRIBUTING DISCIPLINES

This section examines the contribution to MT theory and practice of linguistics (4.4.1) and computer science (4.4.2). Throughout this section, we will occasionally make reference, by way of example, to individual systems. These descriptions are by no means intended to be full accounts, and in some cases may be simplified slightly for the sake of clarity.

4.4.1 Linguistics

In this section we examine the linguistic content of MT, by which we mean both the use which MT makes of linguistics and the linguistic considerations which may affect the design of an MT system. We deal first in general with the kind of linguistic problems that an MT system must resolve, then with the representational matters involved, and finally with methods for deriving representations ('parsing').

4.4.1.1 Problems

We wish here to draw attention to a range of linguistic phenomena which any MT system must address. The reader may be struck by the apparent triviality of some of these problems, but if so should be aware of the human resources that trivialise these problems which are not available in an automated system. In section 4.4.2 we shall consider more closely strategies for resolving some of these problems.

It has been said that the linguistic key to MT is the resolution of ambiguity, and we shall see that most of the problems to be discussed here can be considered as questions of disambiguation of one sort or another. We shall distinguish primarily between 'structural' and 'lexical' ambiguity, in each instance giving readily understandable examples, clarifying the ambiguity by giving a parallel but unambigous example. In each case, the reader should be aware that the necessity to disambiguate is motivated by the requirement to get the correct translation. The section ends with a discussion of some more general problems.

<u>Structural ambiguity</u> Many single words may be more than one part of speech (these are called 'homographs'): when two or more such words occur together in a single sentence, this may result in an ambiguity. For example, in the sentence <u>He saw her shaking hands</u>, her may be a possessive adjective or an accusative pronoun, <u>shaking</u> may be

adjectival or verbal. The constituent her shaking hands is ambiguous between 'her hands which were shaking' and 'the fact that she was shaking hands (with someone)'. If this constituent is subject rather than object, the ambiguity is resolved by subject-verb agreement (Her shaking hands was/were obvious); the same structure with a different word may make one or other reading more obvious (He saw her trembling/holding hands).

In many languages, a relative clause can be considered as a sentence containing a 'gap': the implied filler of this gap can be ambiguous, as in (German) die Frau, die die Magd sah which can mean either 'the woman whom the maid saw' or 'the woman who saw the maid'. The identical structures in die Frau, die die Blume sah ('the woman who saw the flower') and die Blume, die die Frau sah ('the flower that the woman saw') are unambiguous for semantic reasons. A similar ambiguity arises with phrases like the man I want to leave: because leave can be either transitive or intransitive, man can fill either a subject gap ('I want that man to leave') or an object gap ('I want to leave that man').

Gross structural ambiguities may arise not from the ambiguity of one or two constituents, but from different ways of combining constituents. For example, I saw the man in the park with a telescope is three-ways ambigous, depending on whether we understand 'saw with a telescope' (compare I saw the man in the park with my own eyes), 'man with a telescope' (as in I saw the man in the park with a blue shirt), or 'park with a telescope' (e.g. I saw the man in the park with a statue). Coordinations are a regular source of this type of ambiguity: old men and women might mean 'old men and old women', or 'old-men and women-of-all-ages', but compare the unambiguous old men and children.

Notice that all the structural ambiguities discussed in the previous section are essentially monolingual; it may well be that a particular target language has the same ambiguity, as when, for instance, the 'telescope' example is translated into German. But readers who know both German and, say, French, will recognise that this ambiguity is simply a result of an accident of syntax.

Lexical ambiguity   Multiple senses for a single word are common in all languages. We have already seen that when this homonymy corresponds to a difference in part of speech, structural ambiguity may result, though in fact it is usually the case that such homonyms are disambiguated by syntactic context (compare Cowboys round up cattle and He came round thecorner). However, many homonyms are also the same part of speech, and the resulting word-sense ambiguity is more often than not reflected in a different choice of translation equivalent: consider the word board which might mean 'flat work surface', 'playing area', 'committee', 'cost of meals'. Rather similar to homonomy, and not always easy to distinguish from it, is polysemy, or the metaphorical extension of word sense. In the example of board, one could argue that the first two meanings given are 'the same', the second being a metaphorical extension of the first. Unlike homonymy, polysemy is often paralleled in closely related languages, for obvious reasons. The distinction between homonymy and polysemy has been the subject of much debate amongst linguists, but for the purposes of MT it is a side-issue: the main question is whether a given word has one or more possible translations in the target language. If so, then the competing word senses must be disambiguated.

There is a special case of homonymy which only arises in the translation environment, and we can call this 'translingual lexical ambiguity'. This is the case when for a single word in one language there is a choice of translation in another, but this is due to neither homonymy nor polysemy, but to a different richness of vocabulary in a given field. Everyone has heard that the Inuit have lots of different words for 'snow'; by the same token, German distinguishes between inside and outside walls (Wand vs. Mauer), French has a different word for 'river', depending on whether it flows into another river (rivière) or into the sea (fleuve), Spanish differentiates between a human leg (pierna), and a non-human leg (pata), the latter including both animals and furniture. Again, for correct translation the senses must be distinguished, though there is some debate in MT circles as to where this disambiguation should occur: since the homonymy/polysemy is not perceived in the source language, it is perhaps not appropriate or reasonable to expect the linguist involved in the analysis to take it into account.

General problems A number of general problems remain, to which attention should be drawn. In many cases, these arise from the simple fact that languages differ especially in the use of varying linguistic means to express a given cognitive content. An obvious example is the relationship between the concept of time and the use of tense and other linguistic devices to express it: the English simple past tense for instance may need to be translated into French as perfect, past historic or imperfect, depending on context and meaning. Furthermore, where French uses an inflected tense form to express future time, English (sometimes) uses the modal verb will. Other languages - like Chinese - rely more heavily on time adverbials or context to express the implied time reference.

A more serious example of difficulties resulting from use of different linguistic devices can be seen when comparing how English and Russian express definiteness in nominals: in English, a system of articles (the, a, some etc.) is used, whereas in Russian definiteness is partly a function of word-order, e.g. Zhenshchina vysla iz domu ('The woman came out of the house') vs. Iz dom vysla zhenshchina ('A woman came out of the house').

Another problem is the recognition of the antecedents of pronouns: this is often necessary for the correct translation of pronouns into gender languages. Consider the sentence I dropped the glass on the table and it broke: in French, this is J'ai laissé tomber le verre sur la table et il s'est cassé, where il ('it') is masculine in gender like its antecedent le verre ('the glass').

Finally, complex nominals can cause problems, especially when translating between languages which form compound noun-phrases freely, like English and German, and those where relationships between the elements must be expressed more explicitly, like French. So for example there is an important but, in English, hidden difference between alligator shoes and horse shoes.

4.4.1.2 Representation

The linguistic concepts alluded to in this section were introduced in
section 1.2. While it is not to be expected that a framework
developed within theoretical linguistics can be lifted wholesale for
MT purposes, nevertheless an underlying linguistic theory of some kind
is needed. In the absence of such a theory, an MT system will
comprise a mass of <u>ad hoc</u> solutions to ill-defined problems.

The main aim of source-text analysis in MT can be seen as the
construction of an abstract, unambiguous, linguistic representation
which forms a suitable basis for translation. First-generation
systems had essentially no concept of such a representation – or,
rather, it was assumed that the input string itself amounted to such a
representation. The failure of such systems (whatever its other
causes) shows clearly that this assumption is incorrect. An input
string is not a sufficient basis for translation, and must be
subjected to analysis in order to arrive at an adequate
representation. We shall not repeat here the distinction between
transfer- and interlingua-based approaches (see section 4.3.1) and the
distinct kinds of representation which they imply, instead we shall
consider syntactic and semantic representations of texts and the
relations between them.

Syntactic representations may be divided into purely 'surface' ones
and those which are slightly 'deeper' (the reader is warned that our
use of these terms does not correspond exactly to the generative
grammar concepts of 'deep structure' and 'surface structure'). By a
surface representation is meant a phrase structure tree which
indicates syntactic categories and constituency, without in any way
manipulating the input string (i.e., without changing the order of
words). A deeper, more abstract representation might be of various
types: a dependency tree, which explicitly shows relations of
modification and subordination; a phrase structure tree akin to a deep
structure, which makes clear the 'underlying' logical relations of a
sentence; or a surface phrase structure tree augmented by empty nodes
or traces to show the canonical position of constituents (i.e., there
is a kind of pointer from an item's surface position to its canonical
position).

The similarities and differences among these representations may be
illustrated by considering how they would represent and relate the
active sentence <u>This athlete won a medal</u> and its corresponding
passive, <u>A medal was won by this athlete</u>. A purely surface
representation would give the two sentences quite distinct structures
and fail to relate them at all. The deep-structure phrase-marker for
the two sentences would be identical except for a diacritic 'passive':
this diacritic would implicitly carry the information that the surface
structures were distinct by indicating that the deeper representation
had neutralised the differences in word order and verb form. The same
is true of a dependency representation, which would make explicit the
fact that <u>this athlete</u> and <u>a medal</u> were 'deep' subject and object
respectively in both the active and passive sentences. The usefulness
of a phrase-structure tree with traces is seen more clearly in a
sentence like <u>This boy is expected to lose</u>: to the surface
representation would be added a trace showing that <u>this boy</u> is logical
or 'deep' subject of <u>lose</u>.

The deeper representations therefore have the advantage of relating the two strings, and of indicating, in some way, the underlying or logical relations between the verb and the two noun phrases, which are not explicit in the string or the surface representation. Such information may be essential in arriving at a translation for a sentence which cannot be rendered word-for-word in the target language; for instance, This result is believed to be correct cannot be translated word-for-word into French, but must be rendered as an active, On croit que ce résultat est correct (literally 'One believes that this result is correct'). Such examples show that a surface phrase-marker, being a purely syntactic or structural representation, does not form an adequate basis for translation. It is not being argued that a surface representation cannot do any of the work of, say, disambiguation. For instance, it would show different positions for the prepositional phrases in I saw the man with my own eyes and I saw the man with a blue shirt (cf. section 4.4.1.1). But a purely syntactic analysis could have no basis for determining the correct attachments in these examples and, as we have seen, is for other reasons semantically inadequate. The semantic considerations introduced by deeper representations are essential for correct translation.

This should not come as a great surprise. After all, translation is concerned with reproducing meaning: the structure of source- and target-text may, in principle, differ in any way and to any degree, as long as the meaning is transferred accurately. So it is to be expected that a linguistic representation for the purposes of translation will have to contain semantic information.

Among semantic representations, the commonest are those employing 'deep Cases' or thematic relations, such as agent, patient or experiencer. A standard example adduced to show the relevance of deep Case is I like him and its French equivalent Il me plaît (literally 'He pleases me'). Even a deep syntactic representation of these will show I as subject of one and me as (indirect) object of the other (whether or not these functional terms are used explicitly). Only a deep Case based representation can show their cognitive equivalence, with I/me as experiencer and il/him as patient (or whatever) in both. Deep Cases therefore offer a representation which is less tied to the syntactic idiosyncracies of individual languages or individual lexical items than the deep syntactic representations already discussed. It should be noted that this does not mean that deep Case is more suited to interlingua- than to transfer-based approaches.

In addition, there are other translation-relevant aspects of language for which syntactic representations, however deep, are clearly inadequate. One such would be phenomena of time and aspect, since, as we saw above, there is not necessarily a one-to-one relation cross-linguistically between tenses. There therefore needs to be a way of determining the correct tense to use in the target language, which implies some means of representing the temporal reference of the source text, not just showing which tense form is used. Another phenomenon of this type, again seen above, is pronominal reference: a representation which indicates a pronoun's antecedent cannot be regarded as purely syntactic; more importantly, the information needed to establish an antecedent is often semantic (e.g. selectional restrictions or preferences of verbs). In the example where for a sentence like I dropped the glass on the table and it broke to be translated correctly into French, the antecedent of the pronoun it must be established, it is the fact that glasses are more fragile than tables which allows one to determine the antecedent as the glass and not the table.

We have argued, then, that a syntactic representation of a sentence's structure does not provide sufficient basis for translating that sentence into another language. At least some semantic information must be provided as well. The 'as well' is important here: the optimal representation should contain both syntactic and semantic information. For instance, the representation of a passive should not just make clear the logical/Case relations, it should also signify that the sentence is passive: the active/passive distinction should not be neutralised. Even where a semantic representation is provided, knowledge of a string's surface form may be useful for stylistic purposes (e.g. indicating thematisation), and also as a 'safety-net', a kind of last-resort basis for translation if more sophisticated semantic processes fail. It should be added that, although we have implied that a single structure should provide information of different types, it is also possible for a sentence to be assigned more than one representation (e.g. one syntactic and one semantic).

To a large extent, the 'depth' of source-language analysis and the nature of the representation aimed at depend on such matters as whether the system is bi- or multilingual, the degree of similarity of source and target language, and whether the system is interactive, as well as whether it employs an interlingua or a transfer module. There is no single right answer which holds for all systems of all types.

4.4.1.3 Parsing

We now briefly discuss some of the issues involved in choosing ways of manipulating the kinds of representations just dealt with. Target-text synthesis, which involves producing a string of words from some abstract representation is normally seen as a deterministic process, and less attention has been paid to it. As synthesis meets none of the problems of ambiguity which beset source-text analysis, we shall say no more about it here. We also assume that dictionary look-up and morphological analysis have taken place, so that the words of the text already have attached to them information about their syntactic category, subcategorisation frame and inflectional status, and concentrate on parsing, that is to say, going from text to abstract representation (see section 1.5 for an overview of parsing).

One concern of much work on parsing which makes no practical contribution to MT is that of psychological reality. An MT system which intentionally models human translators in that it makes similar errors to theirs is of no use whatever, while a system that models the mental processes of human translators is not an attainable goal at the present time, and in any case adopting such a goal would not necessarily lead to improved translations. It should be noted that the question of modelling the translation process is a separate issue from that of transferring the expert human translator's knowledge to an MT system, which is touched on in section 4.6.

However, other questions which arise in designing any language-processing system are relevant to MT. For instance, given that the desired linguistic representation for MT purposes is an unambiguous one combining syntactic and semantic information, two immediate issues are how disambiguation is to be performed, and how these two types of information are to be related. These issues may usefully be discussed in tandem. Considerations of modularity (see section 4.3.3) would lead one to reject any position which denies a syntax/semantics distinction and builds a semantic structure directly from the input string. Modularity is clearly maintained in a 'sentence-final semantics' or 'two-pass' approach, in which a full syntactic structure is built first and then converted to a semantic representation. One obvious interpretation of this would be to go from a surface syntactic representation to deep syntactic to semantic, using information at each level of representation to construct the next. A big disadvantage of this is that the syntactic module cannot use semantic information to disambiguate, e.g. to decide on the attachment of the prepositional phrases in I saw the man with my own eyes and I saw the man with the blue shirt, as discussed above.

An alternative, obviating this last problem, would be to employ what might be termed 'interleaved' or 'incremental' semantic interpretation: semantic representations are constructed as the parsing process proceeds, on the basis of partial syntactic structures. This need not infringe the principles of modularity and separation: a language's syntax and semantics may be described separately, but the control strategies used by the system may exploit these descriptions in an interwoven manner. In the absence of detailed proposals along these lines, however, the most practical option with regard to global ambiguities may be an approach in which all possible syntactic structures are represented in chart format (see section 4.4.2.3), and semantic considerations are then used to select the most likely reading. As with representations, though, different system designs might call for different parsing techniques.

4.4.1.4 Example

As an example of an operational MT system that involves interesting use of linguistic and parsing techniques, we may cite METAL, the system undergoing development at the University of Texas.

METAL is based on a context-free grammar, and its German analysis component currently contains about 550 phrase-structure rules. Syntactic features (e.g., 'plural' and 'third person') are employed to handle phenomena such as subject-verb agreement. There is also a transformational component, employing transformations which are indexed to specific syntactic rules. Case frames are used in constructing a clause, to help identify a predicate and its arguments.

The computational techniques employed by METAL include a 'some-paths', parallel, bottom-up parser (see section 1.5). It is a 'some-paths' parser, as opposed to an all-paths one, in that it will not necessarily produce all interpretations of an input that are possible with the given rule base. Even so, multiple interpretations will still sometimes be produced by the analysis component, but these will each be assigned a score or plausibility factor. Only the highest-scoring interpretation will go forward as input to the transfer component. This procedure seems to work well, with the highest-scoring interpretation almost always serving as the best basis for translation.

In terms of performance, METAL's German-to-English system appears - on the basis of its developers' claims - to be reasonably efficient. The average time for translation is 5-6 seconds (real time) per input word, and improved hardware could perhaps halve this rate. Up to 85 per cent of the sentences in texts require only stylistic revision by post-editors (though for some texts this figure drops to 45 per cent).

4.4.2 Computer science

In this section we shall consider some of the principles of computer science that have a bearing on MT. In fact, MT encompasses a very broad range of computer science-related activities and is therefore of technical interest even to computer scientists not especially interested in translation or even other areas of language processing. For example, MT typically involves manipulation of large data bases (dictionaries) and data structures; the translation process itself involves a wide range of non-numerical computations of various kinds; and the size and complexity of a typical MT system requires important design and programming decisions to be taken.

The various 'generations' of MT systems reflect not only changes in the linguistic approach, as discussed above, but also different computational views of the problem.

4.4.2.1 Two generations of MT systems

First generation   MT systems of the first generation have been characterised as 'translation programs', and in section 4.3.2 we discussed the important principle of separation of algorithms and linguistic data. It was pointed out above that one of the problems encountered in early MT research resulted from the fact that people working in the field required both linguistic and programming competence: a further disadvantage of this approach was that as MT programs became larger, it became more difficult for any single person to retain a clear understanding of the overall behaviour of the program. This had the undesirable result that attempts to rectify a perceived error in one part of the program often had unforeseen and even untraceable side-effects in another part. A further problem was that often some characteristic of the chosen programming language, which at the time would typically be some rather low-level language, or of the host machine would unduly influence the choice of strategy for solving some principally linguistic problem. It is thus easy to understand why, in the 1960s, when more emphasis was placed on the computer's ability to process large amounts of data rather than on the nature of this processing ('quantity' rather than 'quality'), the approach to MT was in terms of huge dictionary databases with rather simplistic computations.

Second generation   We have described in section 1.5 the advances in computer science which allowed programmers to move away from

programming in low-level code and which led to the design and
implementation of higher-level programming languages and, in
particular the notion of 'syntax-directed compilation'.

Workers in MT have frequently made appeal to the techniques of
compiler construction; this is not, indeed, surprising, given that
compiling can be regarded as a special case of 'translation', i.e. of
one (programming) language into another. In particular, two of the
ideas inherent in syntax-directed compilation were to become very
important in subsequent developments in MT: the notion that a formal
description of a language could be separated out and made to drive a
translation procedure, and the modularity induced by the separation of
the description of constructs in the source language and their
equivalents in the target language.

4.4.2.2 Modularity: structured programming

The notion of structured programming is reflected in the introduction
of modularity in MT systems, as discussed in section 4.3.3.
Modularity, it will be remembered, involves dividing a complicated
computational task into smaller more or less independent sub-tasks
which communicate by means of a strictly-defined interface protocol.
The identification of suitable sub-tasks in second generation systems
is usually a linguistically motivated decision, whereas the definition
of interface protocols is a crucial step involving both linguistic and
computational considerations, to which we shall return below.

One of the advantages of breaking a task down into smaller
components is that this provides a series of obvious and, if the
subdivision of tasks is well motivated, linguistically interesting
'break-points', where the translation process can be halted and the
intermediate results inspected. In this way, testing and development
are facilitated. Furthermore, if some of the sub-tasks correspond to
procedures developed for purposes other than translation, the
appropriate algorithmic solutions to these tasks can be adopted and
adapted: likewise, modules elaborated in the course of development of
the MT system which are useful elsewhere can be passed on. Examples
of such multiple-use packages are plentiful: dictionary look-up
procedures, and any of the components of the analysis or generation
modules. In fact, all but the transfer modules could in theory be put
to other uses.

4.4.2.3 Data structures

In modern computing, problem solving involves not only the design of a
suitable algorithm, but also the definition of appropriate 'data
structures' to accompany the algorithm. As its name suggests, a data
structure provides a structured way of representing data within a
program. In the early days of computing, the only 'data structures'
available corresponded to the physical data structures of the
computer: within the machine itself these would be independent storage
locations in the memory, each one capable of storing essentially one
unit of information or fixed-length sequence of these ('array').
Externally, data could be stored in files: a file represents the
simplest of data structures, consisting of 'records', each of which is

made up of a fixed number of small units of information or 'bytes' - the structure, then, being a componential hierarchy on three levels, in which each element of a given level is made up of elements of the level below.

Early MT systems can be seen to use this data structure explicitly: each translation unit is stored and manipulated on a file, with each record of that file corresponding to a word, punctuation sign or other basic distinctive element. The bytes of each record are used to store associated grammatical information, like category, gender, tense and so on.

With the development of higher-level programming languages came the possibility of defining and manipulating more complex data structures, and the most obvious data structure for MT, as the section on linguistics would suggest, is the tree structure. The essential computational properties of a tree structure can be defined in terms of two primitive relationships: 'dominance' ('A dominates B' = A is above B in the tree), and 'precedence' ('A precedes B' = A is on the same level as, and to the left of, B).

Tree manipulations and traversals can be quite straightforwardly programmed, and the precise use of the tree as a data structure is a linguistic rather than computational question. However, the all-important linguistic question of ambiguity does make itself felt as a computational problem: while ambiguity resolution is an entirely linguistic problem, we are interested here in how to represent ambiguity. Whatever the data structure used, there are two important aspects of ambiguity representation to be considered. First, it must be represented in a way that makes instances of ambiguity easy to identify. Second, and more important, it is highly desirable to represent ambiguity as locally as possible, keeping duplicaton of identical structures to a minimum. Consider, for example, a complex sentence with several embeddings, the deepest of which contains some ambiguity - for example, Alan remembered that Bev said that Caroline thought that chewing tobacco could be dangerous (compare ...drinking beer... and ...drinking water...): although the whole sentence is in a sense ambiguous, it would clearly be undesirable to represent this ambiguity by having several essentially identical representations of the same piece of text, except for the small part of the substructure where the ambiguity occurs: rather, there should be some means of encompassing the local ambiguity locally within a single data structure.

Where a tree is used as the basic data structure, the most obvious solution is to have alternative branches at the appropriate node, representing the two (or more) different interpretations. This makes the whole tree like an 'and/or tree', so that on every branching structure there must be some indication whether the branches represent daughter nodes in sequence ('AND tree'), or alternative mother nodes ('OR tree'). If a combination of true sisters and alternatives is required, considerable complications are involved: for every representational complication there are corresponding complications in traversal and interpretation.

As an alternative, a slightly more complex, but accordingly more efficient data structure was developed, not initially for MT itself, but by researchers in other branches of computational linguistics. This data structure, called a 'chart', consists of sequentially ordered 'nodes' which are linked by arcs or 'edges', each edge being labelled with information indicating the nature of the link. The first and last nodes in the chart have a special status, and there can be no loops in the chart (i.e. an edge conecting a node with either itself or with a previous node). Readers with a computer science background will recognise this as a loop-free directed graph with unique entry and exit points. The structure is developed by adding successive edges which span longer and longer sequences of nodes, the labelling on these edges indicating the internal structure of the node sequence spanned (typically in the form of a tree or, more economically, a trace of the edges subsumed in building the new edge), until at least one edge spans the whole chart, from entry to exit point, labelled with a tree structure for the whole unit. Ambiguity is represented by the fact that there is more than one 'path' from one node to the next. Notice how the desire to localise ambiguity representation is respected: in our example of a · sentence incorporating an ambiguous embedded sentence, both readings of the sentence share the same path through the chart, up to the point of ambiguity, where two paths are possible, these meeting up on the other side, as it were, of the ambiguity. Furthermore, the representation of alternative representations is quite disinct from that of daughter nodes in sequence, so that - for the purposes of disambiguation - ambiguous portions of text can be easily identified as those traversed by alternative paths, i.e. spanned by more than one edge.

In bottom-up parsing (see section 1.5), charts have the further advantage of making it easy to identify and discard partial but unproductive solutions: at the end of processing, any edges that do not form part of a complete path through the chart (i.e. any edges which do not form part of the labelling on the edge spanning the entire chart) are rejected. In top-down parsing with back-tracking (see also section 1.5) on the other hand, partial solutions can be kept for re-use.

Charts have been recognised as a powerful, efficient, perspicuous and flexible data structure for various types of linguistic computation, including MT: indeed a chart is the data structure used in at least two of the more successful operational MT systems in existence (METEO and METAL).

4.4.2.4 Separation: high-level programming languages

In any computing task, the choice of programming language(s) is an important decision, since it is one of the major factors in determining the range of possible solutions to a problem. In the pioneer days of MT, the question simply never arose, since there were effectively no such choices available. However, one of the major outcomes of computer science research has been the development of a huge range of different programming languages with varying aims, properties and associated programming 'styles'. In general there has been a move towards 'high-level' programming languages (HL-PLs), that is, languages which allow problems to be stated and solved in a more 'natural' manner, and free the programmer from the more specific details at the level of the machine itself. They also generally provide not only a more natural metalanguage for stating problems in, but also a set of the most appropriate tools for particular types of problems, and these are the 'data structures' that the programming language provides, or allows the programmer to define. Thus HL-PLs tend to be more oriented towards specific types of tasks than lower-level languages.

Even in these HL-PLs however (among which, for example, Pascal, Lisp, and Prolog are said to be particularly suitable for non-numeric computing), available data structures are underdefined for our own highly specific purposes: data-structure definition facilities are too general, and it is difficult to incorporate specific restrictions, or at best this must be done covertly. This is the situation of having 'enough rope to hang oneself', that is to say, programmers are given so many facilities that they can get themselves too easily into trouble using complex tools where simpler ones would have sufficed. In defining data structures, there is also a need to be able to state restrictions and special properties (e.g. trees with at least one terminal branch at each node; graphs without loops and with unique entry and exit points), and associated operations.

For this reason, there has been a tendency towards the implementation of MT systems using very-high-level task-specific programming languages (VHL-TS-PLs) - often themselves constructed with the use of HL-PLs - in which the basic data structures and associated operations are more deliberately oriented towards those required for MT (as discussed above).

Two existing systems are notable for being based on exactly this principle, and are worth some discussion here.

Q-systems   The METEO system developed by the TAUM group in Montreal is used to translate weather bulletins issued by the Canadian Meteorological Office from English into French. From the point of view of computer science, its interest lies in its implementation, since the entire system utilises a VHL-TS-PL called 'Q-systems', developed specifically for the job by Alain Colmerauer. In Q-systems, the basic data structure is a chart, as described above, and the associated formalism expresses tree-to-tree transductions: operations involve construction or manipulation of tree structures, and the entire translation process is expressed in these terms, that is to say as a sequence of 'rules' which take as input a particular tree structure or sequence of tree structures with associated conditions, and which produce as output data of a similar nature.

It so happens that due to the highly restricted linguistic nature of the texts which METEO translates, this approach is extremely successful. However, there are a number of drawbacks with Q-systems which make them unsuitable for more general-purpose MT. The major drawback is the homogeneous nature of the formalism, which requires all manipulations to be expressed as tree-to-tree transductions. For certain tasks in the translation process, this appears to be rather unwieldy: the formalism is too powerful for some of the more straightforward tasks such as dictionary look-up (which involves pattern matching over a large database), and morphological analysis and synthesis (which is essentially simple string handling). A second problem concerns the question of 'control', which we shall address in more detail later, since Q-systems do not lend themselves readily to the type of 'packaging' implied by the modularity requirement described above.

ARIANE-78   The ARIANE-78 system developed at GETA in Grenoble   at about the same time as METEO meets some of these problems by providing a suite of VHL-TS-PLs, though connected via a common 'interface structure'. The general principle is that the formalisms provided should be no more complex or powerful than is exactly required for the task in question. ARIANE-78 is a classical second generation transfer system, consisting of four VHL-TS-PLs, each with an associated data structure, and corresponding to a specific linguistic process. As each formalism is briefly decsribed, notice how each one has distinct characteristics corresponding to its particular task domain, and consider the extent to which the power and range of each is expressly restricted.

The source text first undergoes morphological analysis including dictionary look-up, for which process the non-deterministic finite-state transducer formalism called ATEF is used. This formalism enables strings to be converted into flat, labelled trees. Because the disambiguation of individual words will be performed later, ATEF produces all possible morphological interpretations. Since finite-state grammars are the most restricted type of formal grammar (type 3 on the Chomsky (1963) hierarchy), they can be implemented with the least complex and most efficient of algorithms.

The resulting flat graph now undergoes 'multilevel analysis', for which the tree-transduction language ROBRA (similar to the Q-systems discussed above) is used. ROBRA permits the definition of transformational rules whose purpose is to build labelled trees of a type familiar to linguists. ROBRA is the most powerful of the four languages that comprise ARIANE-78, and involves complex control mechanisms - to be discussed further below.

The resulting 'interface representation' undergoes a two-stage transfer process: the first involves replacement of source-language lexical items by corresponding target-language items, for which the TRANSF formalism is provided. This formalism is more complex than ATEF, since it allows rules to specify trees rather than strings as input (since lexical transfer may involve consulting linguistic context), but is less complex than ROBRA, since the range of appropriate actions is more limited: no tree transductions are involved, only changes of labelling on branches. The second stage of transfer involves manipulating the source-language trees into configurations appropriate for the target language. As this involves tree transductions, ROBRA is again used.

Generation begins with further tree manipulations with ROBRA: this stage is distinguished from structural transfer on linguistic grounds, tasks being apportioned to one or other module according to the need to take source language information into account.

The final stage of generation consists of converting labelled trees into strings, and is expressed in the tree-to-string transduction formalism SYGMOR. Like ATEF, SYGMOR is a finite-state automaton, but unlike ATEF is deterministic (since for any input there should be only one output).

4.4.2.5 Overall system design

One of the distinctive features of MT systems from a computational
point of view is their size and complexity. Because of this, system
design is of paramount importance, and two aspects of system design
are of particular interest. The first of these, which we shall call
'robustness', concerns the behaviour of the system, particularly with
regard to the consideration that the range of inputs likely to be
submitted to a working MT system may effectively be of unpredictable
complexity. The second concerns the question of 'controlling'
extremely complex sequences of computations in a defined manner so as
to maximise the efficiency of the system.

Robustness   MT systems must be 'robust' in two senses. Bearing in
mind that a general-purpose MT system is never likely to be 'finished'
(one can always expect to be able to improve its performance), it is
necessary that people responsible for the maintenance of the system
must be assured that as they extend its linguistic capabilities, these
additions will not have unforeseen and damaging side-effects
('ripples') on the overall system behaviour. We can call this
'developmental robustness'.

In addition, we also have to consider 'operational robustness'. As
MT systems become more and more unconstrained, incorporating an
extremely wide variety of data structures and operations, it is likely
that they will have the computational power of a 'Turing machine'
(i.e. will be able to perform any imaginable computation), and will
therefore be 'undecidable', that is to say, one cannot be sure that
for any given input the system will terminate and produce some output.
Even before one can be interested in whether the output is appropriate
in some sense, there is the prior worry that, owing to the nature of
the input, the system will simply carry on processing and never
produce any output. When we think of this scenario in terms of a
large-scale MT system, this is obviously an untenable situation:
imagine submitting thousands of words of text to be translated
overnight, and coming back the next morning to find the machine stuck
on the first sentence!

The solution aimed at by MT researchers is to attempt to incorporate
in the system design some way of predicting and recognising such a
situation and reacting appropriately. These are extremely difficult
problems that have occupied some MT researchers for a long time. One
of the approaches suggested is to incorporate devices which recognise
a priori the combination of circumstances that would lead to such a
situation, and to try to minimise these, for example by putting
additional constraints on the type of operation permitted. However,
this restriction of the expressive power of the formalism has the
drawback in general of forcing the linguist to express things in a
contorted or unnatural way merely to meet computationally motivated
requirements. Another approach is to incorporate sophisticated
'control' mechanisms which allow the linguist to divide the task up
into more precise modules, the individual behaviour of which is easier
to ascertain. These mechanisms, which are attractive for other
reasons as well, are discussed below.

A more serious problem of robustness concerns the behaviour of the system when things go wrong. Clearly it is unreasonable to expect an MT system to be able to recognise whether its output is a 'correct' translation: the best one can do is to have a definition of 'well-formed' output. What we are concerned with then is how the system should react once it recognises that it is unable to produce any output conforming to this definition. It is not obvious that this is even possible, but assuming that we can go some way towards this requirement, it is interesting to consider how we would like an MT system to 'degrade gracefully' when encountering, say, a sentence within a large text that it was unable to translate.

There are a number of possibilities to consider: the system could produce no output at all, either omitting the problem sentence from its output, or leaving a gap; or it could leave the sentence untranslated. A more ambitious solution than any of these would be for the system somehow to relax some of the constraints on its well-formedness definition for output and, as it were, produce a second-best output. In this case, it would be helpful to mark such output in some special way, to draw attention to it for the benefit of post-editors. In a highly modular system, each module could have its own well-formedness conditions for output (more on this below), and in the case of failure to meet the conditions for one module, the system could backtrack to the last module whose conditions were met. In the extreme case, this would be the text-input module, in which case the text would be returned untranslated.

<u>Control</u>   One of the ideas behind the concept, discussed above, of separating (or 'decoupling') the linguistic data from the computational algorithms that implement them is that this reflects a parallel separation of the 'declarative' and 'procedural' knowledge in the system. Declarative knowledge consists of facts about the relationships between things, such as the fact that the French noun <u>machine</u> is feminine, or that a noun phrase can consist of a determiner, an adjective and a noun. Procedural knowledge is about what to do with those facts, e.g. if we find a determiner, an adjective and a noun in that order, we can build a representation of a noun phrase. Linguistics has typically been concerned with stating declarative knowledge, whereas computing is often a question of defining algorithms, i.e. bits of procedural knowledge. Even though a rewrite grammar might look like a piece of procedural knowledge, it is not: a rewrite rule in a grammar merely defines a relationship between its left- and right-hand sides. To do something with such a rule, we require the procedural knowledge that says, for instance, of the rule A --> B C, 'if you're looking for A, look for B and C in that order', or 'if you find a B and a C, you have found an A'. What is more, the interaction between the interpretation of individual rules is largely a question of procedural control.

The idea behind separation in MT systems, then, is that linguists should be able to set out their declarative knowledge in a particular formalism, while computer scientists write programs that take that knowledge and do something with it. This arrangement is found in the computational device known as a 'production system', which consists of a set of rules (the declarative knowledge), an interpreter (expressing the procedural knowledge), and a database representing the working space, where the input data are manipulated by the application of the rules by the interpreter to produce the desired output. Several MT systems are explicitly based on this model.

In practice however, it has been found that it is difficult to maintain this strict separation when the set of rules becomes complex, as it is difficult for the linguist to state only declarative knowledge without taking account of the way it is going to be used by the interpreter, as would ideally be the case. In stating only declarative knowledge, the linguist cannot foresee all the possible interactions that will happen at run-time. One possible solution is found in ARIANE-78, where the linguist effectively becomes a 'programmer', using a suite of 'linguist-friendly' programming languages, as we have seen. This idea has been taken a step further in that each module of the system consists of a combination of declarative knowledge, together with a precise description of the way in which this knowledge is to be processed. For example, rules within a module can be applied sequentially or in parallel; the linguist can indicate whether rules should be applied globally, or only to structures created by preceding rules within the module; the sequence of rules in a module may be applied iteratively or once only; and if so, a rule may or may not be allowed to apply to its own output; and so on.

A further way in which the activity of the processor can be controlled, and one which is designed to make the MT system more robust, as discussed above, is found in the CEC's MT system Eurotra, currently being developed, where the linguist states the expected conditions under which a given module is invoked, and the range of expected results of the process defined in it. By strictly defining well-formedness conditions on the input to a module, the linguist is able to control the behaviour of the system by ensuring that no data structures are accidentally operated on by a module intended for some other purpose. In the same way, by defining well-formedness conditions on the output from the module, so that only those data structures produced by the module which conform to this well-defined 'goal' are kept, one can ensure that any other structures accidentally generated ('side-effects') for whatever reason are discarded. The well-formedness conditions also serve to indicate whether the module has successfully terminated: if no well-formed output has been produced, then it is as if the module had not been activated at all. Output conditions for each module may be given in a ranked hierarchy, so that the system can 'relax' its constraints in a well-defined manner, so that 'well-formedness' is not simply a question of 'all or nothing'. Most important of all, the linguist is able to influence the behaviour of the system much more effectively.

4.5 EVALUATION OF MT

Like other tools, MT systems must be evaluated: their effectiveness and cost need to be assessed in order to discover how well they are meeting their users' requirements. Methods of evaluation must themselves meet criteria of efficiency and cost-effectiveness; they should provide useful information at reasonable expense.

With regard to the efficiency of MT, it is useful to distinguish between global and detailed evaluation. Detailed evaluation is concerned with diagnosing the causes of errors, proposing improvements and measuring their effectiveness. As such, it requires lengthy and painstaking work by people closely acquainted with the MT system in question, and is therefore unsuited to discussion in an introductory book. Instead, we shall concentrate on global evaluation of a system's performance.

The commonest criterion in MT evaluation is that of intelligibility. This may be tested by subjecting assessors to a series of questions about the content of the translated text, but this requires some subtlety in setting the questions and evaluating the answers. The simplest and cheapest method is to ask assessors to place the translated text (or each sentence of it) on a scale of intelligibility. The assessors do not have access to the source text, and so do not need to know the source language. The disadvantage is that assessments produced by this method are unable to reveal passages which, though intelligible, are mistranslated.

To assess the degree of fidelity of the translation to the original text requires assessors who know both source and target language. They must consider both original text and translation, which inevitably increases the time, and hence the cost, of the evaluation. Assessors can again place the text, either in its entirety or sentence by sentence, on a scale of fidelity, according to how much of the information in the original is present in the translation. However, the difficulty of determining precisely the content of each sentence makes this criterion less useful than it might appear to be.

Evaluation of intelligibility and fidelity assumes the use of assessors who read the texts specifically in order to evaluate them. A different approach is to ask the end-users of a set of documents whether the translations are acceptable to them. This has the advantage of being inexpensive and of relying on the opinion of the person for whom the translation was made. However, it fails to provide sufficiently detailed information to be really useful.

Merely counting the numbers of grammatical errors in a translation is not very illuminating if done without regard to the implications for intelligibility and acceptability, since a text can contain a number of errors but still be highly intelligible and acceptable. It may be useful to record the number and type of corrections made by a post-editor, but this is bound to be subjective since different post-editors will make different corrections.

Evaluating the cost of MT usually means comparing its cost with that of human translation. A number of distinct parameters must be set before such evaluation can take place: whether the human translation is revised or unrevised; whether or not the machine translation is pre-edited and/or post-edited; the form of the source text (manuscript, typewritten, in machine-readable form, or whatever); the method of production of the target text; and so on. One can then calculate the cost of machine and human translation for a particular body of texts. The original investment in the MT system - whether as a purchase from some supplier, or else in terms of person-years of research and development - must also be taken into account before a valid comparison can be made.

There is, then, no simple answer to such questions as 'how good is MT?' or 'is MT cheaper than human translation?'. Attempts to discover the answers require time, resources and ingenuity, and do not always give straightforward results.

4.6 FUTURE TRENDS

In this final section we assess the current state of the art of MT and look towards its future. In many sections of this chapter we have presented a consensus view, with little or no discussion. In particular we have for the most part submerged our own views where they differed radically from the 'received' opinion. In this section, however, as well as stating what we feel to be the 'accepted' view of where MT is headed, we present a few of our own feelings on the subject.

By and large, when we look at the second generation MT systems (as defined in this chapter) which currently exist, it is difficult to escape the conclusion that they have failed in their objectives. There are, of course, some honourable exceptions, notably METEO, whose success, arguably, is one of the main reasons for the resurgence of MT in the latter part of the 1970s. It is nonetheless noteworthy that METEO operates with an extremely restricted text-type, and that the attempt to generalise its design principles to a linguistically less hermetic class of texts (in the TAUM-Aviation system) had to be abandoned in favour of a more overtly procedural style. Indeed, the only attempt at fully automatic MT to have had any commercial succes beyond systems already conceived during the first generation is METAL, which eschews many of the principles of the second generation (special-purpose programming languages, separation of declarative and procedural knowledge) in favour of a more straightforward, almost 'traditional' approach.

This is not to say that the principles underlying the second generation style of MT are necessarily wrong; it may simply be that they have been applied in the wrong way. In particular, the special languages (VHL-TS-PLs) which characterise second generation systems (Q-systems, ROBRA) were in general motivated by computational rather than linguistic criteria, so that the very expression forms which linguists were supposed to use were simply inappropriate to permit any useful separating out of declarative linguistic knowledge. This is not, in fact, surprising since until the latter part of the 1970s it was a widely held view that linguistic theory and MT had very little of interest to say to each other, while the second generation philosophy had its roots very firmly in the computing practices of the 1960s and early 1970s.

Over the last few years, however, computational and theoretical linguists have taken a new interest in each others' findings. On the one hand, this shows up in a new attention to linguistic theories which, in addition to their linguistic motivation, are suitable for direct computational implementation (such as Lexical-Functional Grammar and Generalised Phrase Structure Grammar). On the other hand, the programming language Prolog, for example, provides a special grammar rule notation which means that grammars written in this notation already are Prolog programs. As yet, few of these advances have found their way into MT, but we can expect that they will become increasingly influential in the future. In particular, the second generation goals of modular systems and decoupled declarative knowledge begin to look much more of a feasible proposition as linguistically interesting notations with a well-defined computational interpretation become available and known to workers in MT.

We have argued in previous sections (4.4.1) that both syntactic and semantic representations are necessary for translation. It is often argued that the next advance in MT - the 'third' generation - will involve the incorporation of pragmatic inferencing or real-world knowledge, thus moving MT closer to the artificial intelligence (AI) paradigm. On this view, the representations of texts should be much farther removed from their surface form and should, for example, make paraphrase and entailment relations of texts explicit. But there is no convincing evidence that representations of the relevant degree of abstractness are suitable - or necessary - for translation purposes, while it is certainly true that the representations in question typically fail to preserve much important information about the syntactic form of the source text. Moreover, this approach carries the implicit assumption that most or all the linguistic problems of MT are solved, which they are not.

Our prediction is that MT will indeed take on board some of the principles and practices of AI, but in a rather different way. One of the most important themes in contemporary AI research is concerned with 'expert systems' - very sophisticated computer programs which can behave in limited domains as an acceptable substitute for a human expert. A major preoccupation in this line of research is with the problem of knowledge transfer: how to provide appropriate tools and notations to allow human experts in the domain to communicate their own knowledge of the domain to the computer. MT lends itself naturally to this kind of treatment: the domain is translation, and the experts are translators, linguists and lexicographers. On this view, the second generation failed predominantly because system architects simply did not provide any natural means of communication between domain experts and the computer.

If this diagnosis is correct, the third generation of MT systems will arrive when we are able to embody in the computer a model of language and translation which is able fully to exploit the enormous fund of knowledge which linguists and translators clearly have. With the recent advances in computational and theoretical linguistics, that time may now be quite close.

4.7 FURTHER READING

Background
Historical surveys like the above have appeared periodically, but, of necessity, can only reflect a contemporary view. Of significant interest, however, are: Hutchins (1978, highly informed and quite detailed), Tucker and Nirenburg (1984), Hutchins (1982), Wilss (1982, pp.228-249) and Lawson (1983) - the last three of these being aimed essentially at the translator.
Of more historical interest are the following: Locke and Booth (1955) (a collection of early articles), Oettinger (1963) and Yngve

(1964) (significant early criticisms), Garvin (1976) and Josselson (1971) (general overviews), Garvin (1972) (a collection of papers), Piotrowski and Georgiev (1974) and Marchuk (1984) (on Soviet MT), Heinisz-Dostert et al. (1979) (three general articles on developments up to the mid-1970s) and Slocum (1984) (an extensive and up-to-date, though perhaps idiosyncratic, overview).

There have been recently several important MT or MT-related conferences and special issues of journals, including the following: CEC (1977), Snell (1979), Lawson (1982), Kittredge (1981a), Loffler-Laurian (1984), King (1985b) and Slocum (1985b).

The principal (readily available) references for the MT systems mentioned in this survey are as follows: SYSTRAN - Toma (1976, 1977), Elliston (1979), Wheeler (1985); TAUM-Météo - TAUM (1973), Chandioux and Guéraud (1981), Kittredge (1981b), Thouin (1982); CETA/GETA - Vauquois (1975), Vauquois and Boitet (1985); SUSY - Maas (1977, 1978, 1985); CULT - Loh (1976), Loh and Kong (1977, 1979); Eurotra - King (1982, 1985a), King and Perschke (1982); MT in Japan - Nagao et al. (1985), and several papers in COLING (1980) and in Horecký (1982); METAL - Slocum (1983, 1985a); Philips/Eindhoven - Landsbergen (1982, 1985); PAHO/Washington - Tucker (1984); UMIST/ICL - Whitelock et al. (1984); Stanford - Wilks (1973a,b).

The Japanese 'fifth generation' is discussed by Feigenbaum and McCorduck (1984). For Q-systems, see Colmerauer (1971).

Modes and uses
Machine-aided human translation: For discussions of this type of approach, see Kay (1980) and Melby (1981, 1983, 1985). See Becker (1984) for multilingual text processing. EPISTLE is described in Heidorn et al. (1982). Information on LOGOS, ALPS and Weidner is available direct from the companies, whose European addresses are: LOGOS, Lyonerstrasse 11, D-6000, Frankfurt 71; ALPs, 14 route du Boudry, CH-2016 Cortaillod NE; Weidner, Fryen House, 125 Winchester Road, Chandler's Ford, Southampton SO5 2DR.

Human-assisted machine translation: See Lawson (1982) for several relevant articles. TITUS is described in Tedd (1979), pp.44ff, and in Barnes (1983), though more recent information might be available from the Institut Textile de France in Boulogne-sur-Seine. Van Slype (1979) discusses post-editing. The interactive system MIND is described in Kay (1973); PTOSYS is described in Somers and Johnson (1979) and in Somers (1983).

Design principles
On the concept of an Interlingua in MT, see Otten and Pacak (1971), Vauquois (1975, pp.142ff), and Hutchins (1978). On the separation of algorithms and linguistic data, see Vauquois (1981). For modularity in computer science see Aho et al. (1974). Multilingualism as a design principle in MT is discussed by King (1982).

The contributing disciplines
Linguistics: For a discusion of homonymy and polysemy, see Chapter 9 of Lyons (1977a). References for the section on representation are the same as those given for linguistics in Chapter 1. For relevant topics in parsing, see Johnson (1983), Mellish (1983) and Ritchie (1983). The linguistic aspects of METAL are described in Slocum (1985a).

Computer Science: Structured programming is discussed in Dahl et al. (1972). A discussion of data-structures which is more or less suitable for the lay reader can be found in Hall (1975), whereas Horowitz and Sahni (1976) is a more advanced treatment. For charts, see Kay (1976) and Varile (1983). Q-systems are described in Colmerauer (1971). ARIANE78 is described in detail in Vauquois (1975) and in Chauché (1975). For more on robustness in MT systems, see Arnold and Johnson (1984). Decidability and computational power are discussed by Minsky (1967). The distinction between declarative and procedural knowledge is found in Winograd (1975). Production Systems are discussed in Newell (1973) and in Davis and King (1977). The idea of control mechanisms for Production Systems is from Georgeff (1982); its development for MT is found in Johnson et al. (1983).

Evaluation
This is discussed in van Slype (1982) and several articles in Lawson (1982).

Future trends
TAUM-Aviation is discussed in Chevalier et al. (1981) and Isabelle and Bourbeau (1985). For Lexical-Functional Grammar see Bresnan (1982), and for Generalised Phrase Structure Grammar, Gazdar et al. (1985). Prolog is described in Clocksin and Mellish (1981). For AI-related MT, see Wilks (1973a) and Chapter 10 of Simmons (1984); researchers at Yale are also working along these lines - Carbonell et al. (1978), Lytinen and Schank (1982). A lay introducton to Expert Systems is to be found in Feigenbaum and McCorduck (1984); a more detailed treatment is given by Hayes-Roth and Lenat (1984) and Buchanan and Shortliffe (1984).

5 Natural language interaction with information systems

In this chapter, we will deal with the impact of computational linguistics (CL) and artificial intelligence (AI) on the design and construction of natural language interfaces to information systems. We choose to discuss this topic largely from one particular point of view, namely that of using natural language to interrogate data bases, given that this area is the primary current focus of activity. Thus, we will be generally concerned with the impact of CL and AI on information science and information retrieval. We shall consider this issue from a monolingual point of view before discussing, in section 5.5, multilingual interfaces to information systems.

5.1 INFORMATION RETRIEVAL SYSTEMS

The classical example of someone requiring information, and interacting with a computer to get it, is that of the user of an information retrieval (IR) system. The aim of an IR system is to try to generate documents which will be relevant to some search statement. Such systems have existed for many years now. They were set up to store representations of documents (e.g. title, author and abstract). Each representation is characterised, usually by a list of keywords, drawn from an indexing language. Thus a collection of keywords assigned to a document could be said to capture (in more or less detail) what the document is about. Each keyword indexes a set of documents, and the query procedure primarily involves combining chosen keywords (via the Boolean operators AND, OR, NOT) in order to output that set of documents which results from the union, intersection or ccomplementation of the sets of indexed documents. Actually such systems are much more complex; we keep to the basic operations here to give the reader a flavour of how they work.

Where, the reader may ask, is the natural language (NL) element, the interaction in NL with the computer? It is a sad fact that very few IR systems pay any heed to NL processing (NLP). We cite an illuminating comment by Montgomery in 1972, which unfortunately still holds true today:

> In theory, the relationship between linguistics and information science is clear and indisputable: information science is concerned with all aspects of the communication of information, language is the primary medium for communication of information, and linguistics is the study of language as a system for communicating information. In practice, however, the relationship between the disciplines of linguistics and information science has not been exploited. (Montgomery, 1972, p.195)

The reasons are partly historical (many IR systems predate interesting work in NLP) and partly a matter of lack of communication. By this we mean that IR researchers have tended to ignore linguistics and computational linguistics, and have preferred to rely on quantitative, probability-based techniques. There is very little intersection between IR and CL as evidenced by the conclusions drawn in the literature during the last two decades. IR systems are document-based, as opposed to knowledge (or fact) based. Many IR systems are closed to the general public, in that people with information needs must address themselves to an intermediary who is trained to help formulate the search and who will then conduct it. So in this, the prime area for NL interaction, there are as yet few instances of NL-based systems, and the signs are that this state of affairs will persist.

Despite this rather pessimistic conclusion, we must be wary of placing all the blame on information scientists. There are some cogent arguments and criticisms to be made concerning work in NLP, and its potential relevance to the two prime areas of the whole information retrieval process, namely NL question-answer interaction, and content analysis of documents. For example, an information scientist will rightly complain that the tradition in CL and linguistics has been, and still largely is, based on the written language, and in particular on the sentence as unit of analysis. This implies that linguistics has little to say about analysing utterances of the type one would expect to find in a question-answer dialogue, and, despite concentrating on written language, can offer few insights into content analysis of an entire text. There appears to have been little movement in linguistics to remedy this situation over the past decade, to the extent that a question posed in 1972, regarding content analysis, has as yet remained unanswered, namely:

> Is the kind of drastic compression of content that must be done to provide a document with an index description a process about which linguists can reasonably be expected to have anything to say? (Sparck Jones and Kay, 1972, p.54)

As a result, information scientists have been forced to develop their own techniques both for analysing documents and for searching for information. The former rely in the main on frequency, statistical and probabilistic techniques, any linguistic techniques employed being, understandably, of a relatively crude kind. The latter can be seen, in simple terms, as involving straightforward operations to manipulate the sets of documents that are indexed by keywords.

A startling battery of automatic techniques for indexing documents was developed over the years. Some experiments concentrated on assigning index terms from a previously manually prepared list. Others investigated how index terms could be automatically discovered in a document. Evaluation of these experiments was not an easy task, as each was based on different criteria and employed a different technique or combination of techniques. However, the evidence supporting some important points is sufficient for them to be taken seriously; thus, the general trend of the experiments ... is to show that relatively simple indexing techniques can be as effective as more complex ones, and that automatic methods of providing simple index descriptions are as effective as manual ones. (Sparck Jones and Kay, 1972, p.126)

In the early 1970s, it was found that anything more complex than simple keyword weighting or the use of a simple thesaural structure to bring in related keywords proved to be either not worth the extra effort, or indeed counter-productive. These results still held good in the latter half of the decade and do so still in great measure today.

As regards querying an IR system, because of the nature of the data base (sets of documents, each set indexed by a keyword), there has been little need felt for NL analysis of queries, as these can be expressed in terms of keyword combinations and Boolean operators (and other devices we omit here) with a level of precision adequate for retrieval of relevant material. For a variety of reasons (knowledge of how certain documents are indexed, familiarity with the structure of individual data bases, proliferation of query languages, etc.), IR systems are commonly directly accessed only by intermediaries.

It would seem, then, that information science has been able to cope quite adequately without sophisticated linguistic techniques.

However, all is not well within this discipline, and there is another, major reason for the lack of interaction between information science and linguistics (and its related disciplines), stemming from the theoretical basis of information science itself. It has been pointed out that the conceptual foundations of information science are not well established, and that in particular, there is a lack of agreement about just what 'information' is. Furthermore, there is a corresponding lack of knowledge about the relationship between a user and the 'information' contained in a document retrieval system. Such a state of affairs would tend to call into question the whole philosophy of IR systems, especially the emphasis on the use of keywords. Perhaps it is timely to consider ways in which collections of documents might be more usefully organised and exploited.

We said above that IR systems are document-based, not knowledge-based. If, however, we consider the needs of users, it becomes clear that what most users want today is precise information. People do not have time to read primary or even secondary sources. In an IR system, precision is not so important, as it is the human who performs the final selection of material. In other words, an IR system can afford to be imprecise, for the user does not expect high precision. Further, the keyword indexing method cannot but be imprecise when used on a large scale in a system with many different types of user, especially if keyword assignment is performed by a large number of human indexers. Increasingly, though, users will be demanding systems which deliver facts. In such a system (a question-answering (Q/A) system), precision is of the utmost importance. The user does not expect to get a list of references to documents to help potentially fill the information need. Instead, the user expects to get a straight, precise answer to a question, and does not expect to be suspicious of a system's responses. The difference lies in responding to questions with factual answers, and responding to queries with a set of references likely to lead to a factual answer. As soon as we start looking at knowledge-based systems, then we find ourselves back in the area of NLP.

For us, a knowledge-based system is one which consists not of a (perhaps structured) collection of documents, but of a structured set of elements of information. A knowledge base is then an integrated whole, whereas a document base is a collection of discrete documents. In fact, one could imagine a knowledge base being built up from a collection of documents, each of which is analysed to extract the information it contains. Indeed, early researchers predicted with confidence the design and development of systems which would build up factual information based on document analysis, and which would converse with the user while he formulated his search request. This leads us into a discussion of question-answering systems.

5.2 QUESTION-ANSWERING SYSTEMS

From the viewpoint of the relation between the NL processor and the data stored, Q/A systems may be divided into two types:

1 Integrated systems. By an integrated system we mean that the NL processing is inseparable from the structures of the information store, i.e. that the data structures are conceived with the NL processor in mind, and/or vice versa.

2 So-called front ends, which can be plugged on to the 'front' of a range of data retrieval systems to provide an NL interface. These front ends will analyse a user request, and as it were 'translate' the request into a statement of the particular data base query language being employed. This statement will then be handed to the data base management system (DBMS). As far as the DBMS is concerned, it has received a valid request in its own language – it knows nothing of an NL analyser.

Current research is directed mainly towards type 2 systems, for several reasons:

1 Today there is a realisation that much effort is needed to construct NL processors, and that therefore we should avoid having to reconstruct from scratch for every new data base application.
2 Data bases of all kinds, not just document bases, are becoming more widespread, and being accessed by more people, therefore rapidly customisable NL interfaces are highly desirable.
3 With advances in system design and CL, we can now find general solutions to problems that previously required specific, idiosyncratic solutions.
4 A particular data base model, the relational model, is becoming more popular. It is therefore becoming economically feasible to

construct front ends that can interface with this class of data base. More importantly, the relational data base is based on formally well-defined concepts, relations and operations, and hence it becomes a fairly straightforward matter for an NL interface to compose a search statement.

Type 1 systems have the advantage of being data base specific, and hence able to be specialised for the structures and contents of the data base they are part of, such that higher performance may be achieved. Early Q/A systems were of this type, and there are still systems being constructed today like this. However, in the world of commercial data bases, they are being ousted by the more portable type of system (i.e. type 2). It is still the case though that in the field of artificial intelligence (AI) such interfaces are commonly found as integral components of expert systems, largely due to the fact that AI knowledge bases tend to be of widely diverse types.

5.2.1 Characteristics of Q/A systems

Although two main types of Q/A systems exist, they have much in common. In this section, we will ignore the basic differences, and present in general terms the characteristics of a Q/A system.

Often, a Q/A system will attempt to deal with only a subset of a NL. Note that the very name 'Q/A system' implies that what the system expects as input from a user is something in the form of a question. In a normal dialogue, there are many kinds of utterances. Most Q/A systems will find it difficult to cope with the full range of human expression: they tend to deal with only those grammatical structures that are predominant in the specialised domain of their discourse, on the principle that one can achieve very good results if one deals with a limited syntax and a limited vocabulary. By choosing a circumscribed environment (referred to as a 'microworld'), the Q/A system designer can then exclude many concepts and relations and so construct a system that will not agonise over utterances that are ambiguous in the wider context. Dictionaries and grammars associated with a limited domain system will be smaller by comparison with a more general system, and consequently faster responses may be elicited. With a restricted system, many of the knotty problems of discourse can be quietly ignored, and prompts can be given to lead the user to supply clearer input. Thus there is no great need to attempt analysis of conjunctions, quantification, polysemy, ellipsis or anaphora. If necessary, in an interactive situation, a system can enter into a 'meta-dialogue' (i.e. a dialogue about the dialogue) to ensure the user ends up by asking the question in a form the system can understand.

There is another reason for the common choice of a microworld environment for a Q/A system, namely, that AI knowledge representation techniques are in an early stage of development, such that they are presently unable to handle the vast quantities of knowledge that are essential for macroworld environments. A further problem is that inference and deduction research is likewise in its infancy, so that in a macroworld environment there can be no efficient or even possible way of achieving an unambiguous representation of a query. This accounts for the fact that many of the systems reported in the literature are prototype, experimental systems, able to handle only a small amount of information. Such prototypes demonstrate or investigate knowledge representations or deductive techniques, in the hope of contributing to the gradual accumulation of solid research and the development of more general systems.

Those researchers who concentrate on general, macroworld knowledge representation often do so through a desire to design and test models of human cognition. The objectives of designers of Q/A systems are radically different, as they are not primarily, or even secondarily, concerned with simulating or emulating human cognitive processes. Rather they wish to facilitate communication between human and machine, by allowing them to interact using natural language. Thus there is less emphasis on designing a system that could be said to 'understand' in a deep cognitive sense, and more concentration on helping a user by responding to queries in such a manner that not only is the information need filled, but the user feels satisfied with the advice offered. The user is not interested in whether the system understands the query, but simply wants an answer. From the designer's point of view, it is not necessary that the system understand completely, only that it achieve as full a picture as it can get of the user's information need, which can then be transformed into a request to the knowledge base. This does not, however, preclude a desire to model the user's current beliefs, concerns, views and general state of knowledge about the subject area being investigated.

It has been demonstrated that expert users of Q/A systems who know the special subject, are familiar with the contents of the data base, and are used to expressing themselves in the special language of the field, can achieve a high response rate. Non-expert users, however, tend to get much lower response rates as they will adhere to the rules of general language discourse. Thus there is a clear dividing line between expert and non-expert users, and it would be useful for a system to be able to detect when it was dealing with an expert, and when not, and attempt to correct the situation either by compensating automatically (which is probably a difficult task), or by simply interacting with the user to guide them into expressing themself in a way more likely to achieve better results, as mentioned above. This is but one aspect of the problem however, and is a direct result of human ignorance of the rules of special language discourse.

More serious is the case, common to both expert and non-expert user, where a user may have an incomplete understanding of their information need, or may actually believe some fact to be true when it is not. In such a situation, it is necessary for the system to have access to a model of the user's beliefs, so that it can then point out to the user the erroneous nature of some belief, and moreover force a change in those beliefs to enable mutual beliefs to be held. In fact, the system would have to engage in continuous modelling throughout a query session, as it can have no way of knowing beforehand what the status of the user's beliefs is, or how they will be affected by the results of queries. Therefore modelling the user's behaviour and beliefs assumes critical importance in Q/A systems which aspire to a high degree of helpful advice, rather than the unintelligent regurgitation of facts, leaving the user to sort them out as best they can.

5.2.2 Types of knowledge required for question-answering

We cannot at present conceive of an off-the-shelf stand-alone front end to interface with a complex knowledge base. This remains a topic for future research. The main reason for this is that there is no uniform representation for knowledge available. Although much work has been done in the field, we still remain with only vague notions of what a general knowledge representation would be like. There can therefore be no general solution to the problems of question answering where a system needs to have access to complex knowledge in order to generate inferences leading to specific answers. Nevertheless, a lot is known about the various types of knowledge needed for question answering. Some of the more important types of knowledge are:

1 Subject or topic knowledge: the system must know about the concepts, terms, expressions, special syntax and semantics of the subject field (or microworld) it is oriented towards.

2 Common-sense knowledge: the system must have access, broadly speaking, to things that every human knows.

3 Knowledge of focus: the system must be able to detect the focus of a conversation, to enable proper resolution of anaphora, ellipsis, etc. Furthermore, changes in focus must be detected.

4 Linguistic knowledge: in addition to general linguistic knowledge, the system must be especially capable of dealing with the various types of ambiguity that crop up, for, as has been mentioned in earlier chapters, ambiguity resolution is one of the hardest tasks to accomplish. Normally, this is considered difficult at the level of normal written text. The problems are compounded when attempts are made to analyse discourse. The main types of ambiguity that have to be resolved are syntactic and lexical ambiguity. However, there are other, perhaps more pernicious types, such as ambiguity of Case roles (cf. the role of the preposition on in the sentence He put his report on the table on the stroke of twelve) and of pronoun reference. It is relevant that the use of pronouns is far more common in discourse than in written text. Also, large amounts of real-world knowledge may be needed to find the correct reference. Finally, there is a type of ambiguity which can pose severe problems, namely that between a literal and an indirect meaning. It is often not clear, even from surrounding context, whether a literal or indirect interpretation is called for, and either will often be both possible and correct. Thus the question Can you close the window? admits two interpretations, one giving rise to a yes/no answer, the other to compliance/non-compliance to a request. Even if a system is given some capability to understand the pragmatics of discourse, the wrong interpretation may be made. That is, it is easy to think of a situation where a user merely wants to know whether the system can in fact accomplish some action rather than to receive a print-out, as in the question Can you list all ships currently in their home port? or Can you handle relative clauses? (i.e. implying 'or is this not something you can handle?').

Besides having to possess the above-mentioned types of knowledge, a requirement of a good general Q/A system is that it be capable of accepting all kinds of non-standard or deviant input. Again, we talk of deviance from the norm of written text, largely because the analysis of discourse phenomena is not advanced enough to allow us to characterise precisely a norm for discourse. An extreme position is that there is no norm for discourse, and that more or less anything that can be said goes. Thus a user may supply some input which displays highly unusual word order, where key function words are missing and which terminates abruptly resulting in a fragmentary utterance, for example:

Manchester Paris early on Saturdays flights or maybe London

The user will expect the system to react in a reasonable manner, to deduce what is meant and to supply the answer wanted, just like a human interlocutor would. Furthermore, the next input may be highly elliptical, referring to the previous input. As we have said, such input will be either quietly ignored by the Q/A system that is restricted to a sub-language, or the user will be asked to re-express it in a more acceptable form. However, a general-language, general-purpose Q/A system will have to cope with such utterances somehow, without engaging in a 'meta-dialogue' which will tend to alienate the user.

Other obstacles to smooth processing are more tractable, such as spelling errors, the use of new words not in the system's dictionary, and the use of common circumlocutory or phatic phrases common to human discourse ('I wonder if you would be so kind as to inform me of the fact whether...'; 'By the way, ...'; 'If it's possible, please ...'; 'Hi, how are you, tell me ...'). False starts alone present a considerable obstacle ('Move the red block on to the floor and ... no, the blue one').

All the above concerns form the subject matter of what is known as robust processing, that is, causing the system to continue even when presented with input that it may consider ill-formed. Without such a capacity, a Q/A system will rapidly alienate its users, who will be unwilling to restrict their normal mode of expression (together with all that entails) to adapt themselves to the system's requirements and expectations.

Much work has consequently been going on in this area; however, we are unable to expand upon this subject here, and must be content to refer the interested reader to some recent research, details of which are given at the end of this chapter.

The problems discussed above relate mainly to the analysis of user input. Let us look briefly at the corresponding area of generating system output. Although in the past this area received less attention, today it is assuming greater importance. With the development of more sophisticated analysis components, there has come a desire better to employ the retrieved results. However, this whole area suffers from severe problems of control. That is, it is in the interests of the Q/A system designer to construct a system that will provide succinct, terse and brief answers. Mere exhaustive regurgitation is not what is wanted in most cases, yet it is difficult to conceive of non-ad hoc strategies for limiting the stream of output information. A system trying to be helpful by providing extra information in the form of answers to anticipated questions may deluge the user with unwanted, spurious information. On the other hand, too terse answers are just as unhelpful, involving the user in protracted dialogues to elicit the desired information.

What is at issue here, and in other cases such as those involving misleading or unexpected responses, is the 'principles and practices of standard conversation'. In a dialogue with a computer, people will use strategies for interpreting its output that they will normally apply to responses from other humans. Their expectations will likewise be affected. Computer generated responses should then take these strategies and expectations into account, so that the user will not be misled.

The most successful Q/A systems are those that deal with a microworld, and embody quite severe constraints on the nature of the query language (i.e. the subset of NL) permitted and on the type and scope of inferences that may be performed. The price to be paid for this success is a high one, as inevitably a custom-designed interface cannot be easily transported to another, different data base. Currently, there are few Q/A systems that can approach any level of generality of application. In order to achieve a level of generality of application, a prerequisite is a detailed knowledge and understanding of the whole nature of question-answering. We are still a long way from reaching this desirable state of affairs, although there have been some noteworthy attempts at providing portable Q/A systems, for example the SRI DIALOGIC project offshoot named the TEAM system, and the LIFER system, discussed in section 5.4.

5.2.3 Current research in Q/A systems

An active area of study is that of enabling Q/A systems to provide additional informative comments in a motivated fashion, by allowing them to 'take the initiative' in a dialogue, and provide more information than strictly asked for. We will look at five types of initiative that have received attention in recent years.

5.2.3.1 Signalling incorrect presuppositions of the user

It is often the case that users may harbour some misconception(s) about the information they are seeking. Today's conventional Q/A systems do not disabuse users of their misconceptions, and in fact may reinforce them by delivering a misleading response (including the NIL or NONE response which is highly ambiguous in that it can mean: no information available; the system cannot handle this query; partial information only available; and ...). Furthermore, due to uncooperative responses, a user may develop other misconceptions or become hopelessly confused as to the proper state of things. Recent research distinguishes two broad types of misconception that may arise, namely misconceptions about what is the case, and those about what can be the case. The former are the type that have received most

attention in the literature; however, work in this first area has had
the beneficial effect of highlighting other types of misconception.
The latter type of misconception, about what can be the case, can be
subdivided into at least two types. The first involves
misunderstanding about the constraints on relations and entities in a
data base: thus a request for information on students who teach
courses, for example, would signal a user misconception to the system,
given that the relation 'teach' could not hold between the entity type
'student' and the entity type 'course'. The second subtype concerns
constraints between events and states and their relationship over
time. That is,

It is possible for a user to be mistaken about what can be
true now or what could have been true (or happened) in the
past, (1) because s/he is unaware of the occurrence (or non-
occurrence) of some event or of its consequences or (2)
because s/he believes some event has occurred when it hasn't.
(Webber and Mays, 1983, p.651)

A good Q/A system, then, should not only give cooperative responses
which will be clear and helpful enough to prevent misinterpretation,
but should be able to detect when a user is possessed of some
misconception and be able to remedy it.

5.2.3.2 Offering to monitor for the requested information

In the case that a system cannot provide a useful response, because of
a lack of information, it should offer to contact the user when it is
in a position to give a helpful answer. This function, while a
relatively simple one, would help to extend the usefulness of a
system, and would contribute greatly to making systems more user
friendly. An offer to monitor for information can also arise as a
result of detection of a misconception regarding the timing or
occurrence of events, and so monitoring must be seen as closely
related to the identification of user misconceptions. We said above
that monitoring is a simple function, however this is only so on the
surface. In order to be able to monitor properly, a system must be
able to recognize what events are really possible:

User: Is the John F. Kennedy within 30 miles of LA?
System: No, but shall I let you know when it is?

User: Is Santa Cruz within 30 miles of LA?
System: No, but shall I let you know when it is?

(from Webber et al., 1983)

5.2.3.3 Signalling discontinuities

Discontinuities constitute a major problem of Q/A systems. A
discontinuity arises if, when one of the parameters of a query is

varied, a significantly different answer is produced which the user may well have wanted to know. Examples have been drawn from a study of the way travel agents go about calculating fares. They tended to give the exact cost of a flight for the dates expressed, but would not inform the client of the advantages of travelling some days earlier or later to take advantage of seasonal changes in fares. It has been maintained that a responsible Q/A system should be capable not just of giving an exact answer in response to a query, but also of telling the user that other possibilities exist. On the other hand, there may be so many candidate discontinuities that the system will suffer severely from combinatorial explosions.

5.2.3.4 Justifying responses

Justifications should be produced as an integral part of any system, as people must often take vital decisions based on a computer's response and so should be provided with ample justification to allow them to accept or reject that response. Two major problems in this area are: how to design a system to give justifications in a succinct way, i.e. to say no more than is necessary, which can be seen as a problem of control; and how to provide the user with a well-structured justification. Note that a justification is not necessarily the same thing as a sequence of logical proofs. Proofs are useful to help achieve a response; however, an explanation or justification of a response is often given by humans in terms of an overall strategy that does not consist of a set of proofs.

5.2.3.5 Anticipating follow-up questions and gauging the impact of additional comments

The IMP system is an experiment to gauge the assumptions and expectations of a user, and to make additional comments according to their anticipated impact on the user's impressions. In particular, the system tries to assess the impact on the user of its having failed to make certain comments. Further, it can appear to be positively or negatively biased in its answers, depending on how it calculates the user's attitude towards it. The designer of the IMP system also worked in connection with one of the better-known systems, namely the HAM-ANS system, which has had a large degree of success. There are many aspects to HAM-ANS, but we shall mention only one here, as being relevant to our present concerns. Recent work on this system has been devoted to increasing its already impressive capabilities, especially by giving it the capacity to anticipate follow-up questions. That is, attempts are being made to improve upon the simple, direct responses of a conventional Q/A system, in favour of more cooperative responses which go beyond question answering by supplying what are now known as extended responses. Many yes-no questions must pragmatically be interpreted as indirect wh-questions. Thus if the following question is put to a version of HAM-ANS which is an interface to a vision system: 'Has a yellow car gone by?', the system will interpret this as an indirect wh-question and give the answer: 'Yes, one yellow one on Hartungstreet.'

In supplying this extra, more specific, information, HAM-ANS has recognised that the user in fact wants more information than merely a yes/no answer to a simple question. Given the pragmatics of question answering, it is unlikely that the user wishes merely to know whether a car has gone by. Normally, a human interlocutor would respond with the extra information. With a conventional Q/A system, the answer would be 'Yes', requiring the user to formulate other more specific questions to find out where in fact the car had gone by. The pragmatics of question answering are closely related to the cognitive processes involved in determining the truth value of propositions (i.e. in the present case, 'whether a yellow car went by'). They show that in order to verify that a car has gone by, the spatial location of this event must of necessity be determined. As a side-effect of finding out whether a car has gone by, the information as to where this event happened is then made available. Providing this type of extended response in HAM-ANS can then be seen as a function of filling out case role slots automatically while searching for the correct (simple) answer or indeed detecting empty case slots and seeking to fill them in expectation of providing further information. HAM-ANS provides further information of the extended response kind by using more specific quantifiers in responses than present in the queries, and by generating explicit partial answers to both parts of coordinated queries, as shown in the two following examples (from Wahlster et al. (1983)):

Q. Have several vehicles stopped on Biberstreet?
A. Yes, two.

Q. Have a station wagon and a truck driven away along Biberstreet?
A. No, one station wagon, but no trucks.

There are, however, difficult questions of control to address, in order to prevent, for example, the listing of a long series of streets on which a car had driven by.

5.3 Q/A SYSTEMS, CONVENTIONAL DATA BASES AND KNOWLEDGE BASES

We have looked briefly at IR systems, and at Q/A systems in some greater detail, concentrating on the user-machine interface, and largely ignoring the characteristics, or the role, of the various types of data base. Recall that we said at the outset of section 5.2 that Q/A systems fall into two categories - integrated and front-end systems.

A classification of Q/A systems due to Karlgren is a useful one, as it helps to explicate further the notions of 'front-end Q/A system' and 'integrated Q/A system'. He distinguishes systems based on simple processing techniques from those demanding more sophisticated ones. His classification further points out the importance of knowing the relative finiteness of the sets of questions and answers.

What he calls 'Type 1' Q/A systems are those which treat a finite set of questions, typified by airline reservation systems, i.e. many standard commercial data base systems. Such a Q/A system is (he demonstrates) a convenience device, for if all possible questions are known a priori, it would be a trivial matter to assign answers to them, once and for all, and provide simply a list of questions and their answers. Opting for a Q/A system instead of such a list is therefore a means of providing a more efficient service. No understanding is required of such a system.

'Type II' systems are exemplified by the typical IR document-retrieval system, which embodies a finite set of answers. That is, the set of possible answers is the set of all subsets of the set of document references. Remember that an IR system will combine and divide sets of documents to yield a final set hopefully able to satisfy an information need. In principle, then, there is a finite number of combinations possible.

'Type III' systems correspond to the general Q/A system, characterised by the capability to generate an infinite set of answers. It is necessary for such systems to have a measure of understanding, to be able to reason, to perform inferences and to draw analogies. In contrast to Type I and II systems, a Type III system cannot foresee the set of possible questions. Nor can it generate a finite set of answers, for the important reason that it does not store discrete elements such as document references. Rather, the structured knowledge it contains is used as a basis for answering a question. Furthermore, the complete answer will depend on information gleaned by the system from an analysis of the input question.

It would appear, according to Karlgren, that for Types I and II the actual Q/A component could be of the front-end variety, whereas for Type III this would be far less likely. That is, a system requiring a large amount of understanding is more likely to employ data structures custom-designed for the Q/A application, in other words be more akin to a knowledge base, whereas a more limited system could simply exploit conventional data structures.

Let us look more closely now at the relationship between conventional data bases and knowledge bases.

The existence of two different types of Q/A systems (i.e. integrated systems and front-end systems) is, in part, due to the large gap that exists between AI data base researchers and researchers in conventional data base theory and design. While each set of researchers is concerned with representing information, and making that information available in interesting ways, there is a radical difference in the way each views the information to be processed and manipulated. The former are concerned with elaborating knowledge bases, that is, they see a data base as a representation of the world of knowledge. In a strong sense, a knowledge base represents an interpretation of the stored information, in terms of some chosen high-level representation, or conceptual model. On the other hand, a conventional data base designer has eminently practical ends in view, namely to achieve an efficient organisation of very large amounts of information according to some rather low-level data model, in terms of complex file organisations, a set of data structures and associated operations to manipulate the data base. Further, there is a concern with efficient retrieval, security, and multiple user views. A conventional data base, implemented according to some data model (relational, hierarchical or network, to mention the three standard models), and which is meant to admit different views of the data, by definition must remain neutral, i.e. must not be oriented towards one (or any) interpretation of the stored data. Mylopoulos makes the point succinctly when he says

A database stores (large amounts of) data. In the case of databases, there is no commitment to an interpretation of the information stored in the database; for knowledge bases, on the other hand, there definitely is such a commitment. (Mylopoulos, 1983, p.1202)

Database designers are furthermore more machine-oriented, in that, despite wishing to ensure that the data base remains neutral with respect to any interpretation (hence, one would think, more abstract), they are concerned primarily with storing data on a machine according to one particular model. All subsequent views are then handled in terms of this logical model. On the other hand, a knowledge base designer has chosen deliberately to devote attention to viewing the world of knowledge in a particular way, without being concerned about lower-level machine considerations.

These two approaches, the knowledge base one and the conventional data base one, are radically different, and proponents of each have little common ground between them. However (as Mylopoulos points out) there are ways in which the two sets of designers could and should interact, with mutually accruing benefit. If we look at conventional data base technology, we see that it is accustomed to handling large amounts of data efficiently, and is closely concerned with problems of actual implementation. AI data base technology, on the other hand, is currently capable of handling data bases of a very limited size, and moreover makes few concessions to efficiency of implementation. In many ways, 'implementation' is a dirty word to an AI data base researcher. The main point made by Mylopoulos and his co-workers is that the two domains should interact, as each can learn from the other, and contributions from each can lead to improvements in the other. Thus, in the first instance, conventional data modelling techniques may well be of useful application in the AI world, and AI techniques can be used to aid the task of the conventional data base builder.

There is a wider perspective on the horizon, however, namely the merging of the two technologies, such that data base designers can benefit from AI expert systems like data base generators. A designer would then give a specification of a data base to a generator, which would automatically produce the required implementation. Furthermore, AI technology could help to provide tools that will enable knowledge bases to be easily and rapidly described and further will allow this description to be implemented in the form of one or more data bases. In other words, why not bring together the high-level conceptual view of AI knowledge bases, and the low-level logical view of conventional data base design, and recognise that they are in fact two extremes on the data base design continuum? The various tools, generators and expert systems that are envisaged would typically incorporate the knowledge of an expert data base designer, and that of an expert knowledge base designer.

A major stumbling block to this whole enterprise of marrying the two technologies, however, is the enormous bulk of data to be processed, stored and manipulated by real life applications. To take the case of a document retrieval system, this typically deals with huge numbers of documents (even when documents are represented by some surrogate such as an abstract, there are still huge numbers of abstracts), each of which must be analysed to discover its content, and assigned keywords to characterize it sufficiently to allow for efficient retrieval. The human effort required to index documents for retrieval is non-trivial and there is a wealth of literature on the subject, as it is central to the whole task of information retrieval.

From this brief review of the concerns involved in producing a compact description of a document sufficiently rich to enable useful retrieval, we can appreciate the amount of processing needed for even a modest IR data base. We must also remember that automatic indexing methods are not widespread. For a full-scale Q/A system with a knowledge base, such as those being heralded as the new generation of information systems, the problem of size becomes even more acute, because now we must store not a compressed description of a document (in the shape of a list of keywords) but all the facts contained in the document, together with their relation to other facts in the base. For a non-trivial, real-life knowledge base, there must exist efficient ways of capturing the content of a document (the facts therein) and of incorporating new with existing information.

To sum up, there is an intimate relationship between Q/A system (or NL interface) and the data base it is attached to. Furthermore, it is now recognized that conventional data bases and AI knowledge bases can be viewed not as totally separate objects, but as points on a continuum of data base types, and more importantly, that better examples of each can be constructed using techniques drawn from the other. With this new perspective, we must reappraise the role and function of Q/A systems. Before doing so, however, we will present in section 5.4 short studies of some of the better-known systems. Our survey is of necessity limited, given the scope of this book, and we suggest that interested readers should consult the primary literature. Here, we emphasise important or novel features, to give readers an appreciation both of the capabilities of these systems, and of their design and operation.

Note that we make no reference to early Q/A systems, even though some of these, e.g. LUNAR, are considered important milestones in the development of Q/A techniques. We have concentrated on current or recent systems in an attempt to show what is feasible and what remains to be done. In our conclusion, which follows this section, we will come back to our reappraisal of the role of Q/A systems, once the reader is a little more familiar with their present capabilities.

5.4 EXAMPLES

5.4.1 PLANES

PLANES is an English Q/A system of the front-end type, for a large relational data base containing maintenance information on US Navy aircraft. It is therefore concerned with a limited domain, and can take full advantage of knowing a priori the vocabulary to be used. Furthermore, with a limited domain, the system can predict, as it were, the range and type of sentences (or queries) that will be commonly used by the user population, and safely deal only with these. Treatment of some domain-specific forms of ellipsis is possible, as is treatment of a few general patterns for embedded clauses typical of the special language of this subject. The efficiency of the system is further improved by carrying out spelling correction before the main analysis phase. Of main interest in this system is the small importance of syntactic information. That is, PLANES makes little explicit use of such information, preferring to scan the input with the objective of discovering semantic units that can be mapped more or less directly into some formal query statement. Indeed, the role of surface syntax in this system is largely reduced to providing an ordering for the semantic constituents that are discovered in the input sentence. Thus, the system will try to identify units of input as instantiations of the general semantic concepts it 'knows' about, using a variant of Case grammar (see section 1.2). One of the standard 'concept Case frames', in simplified form, is

QWORD MAINTTYPE MAINTACTION PLANETYPE TIMEPERIOD

This string of semantic constituents would then match the input query

What maintenances were performed on A7's in June 1971?

Now, there is an important consequence of largely ignoring surface syntax: the system is able to deal with syntactically ill-formed input, i.e. non-standard written English. In fact, it was a design decision of PLANES to expect queries expressed using the facilities of normal discourse (ellipsis, anaphora, lack of articles, deletion of verbs, etc.), but which would be semantically well-formed. Writing a syntactic analyser to cope with the wide range of variation in discourse was deemed to be too large and complex a task.

Although a model of its kind, PLANES did have some drawbacks. For example, a strict adherence to the perceived vocabulary of the sub-language meant that certain acceptable queries could not be answered. Thus, the system is restricted to analysing 'make' as a flying action, while 'perform' is always interpreted as involving some maintenance action, as in the following

1 How many flights did plane 3 make in June?
2 How many maintenances were performed in June?

Any other usage of make or perform' is not recognised, for example as in the following

1 How many flights did plane 3 perform in June?
2 What maintenances were made on A7's in June?

processing of semantic units as independent entities, it cannot attempt any further analysis of, say, <u>make</u> to determine the appropriate sense of the verb. Tennant (1981) points out these, and other, deficiencies of this system. Judged overall, though, PLANES is a successful Q/A system, whose design has greatly influenced more recent work in the field. JETS is the successor to PLANES.

5.4.2 LIFER

LIFER was designed to provide an off-the-shelf utility for building Q/A front ends which could then be applied to a particular domain. That is, instead of being provided with a ready-written front end that is specialised towards an application, a user receives an 'empty' skeletal system, comprising a parser and a set of interactive tools allowing rapid development of a sub-language specification. The user then specifies an 'application language', which embodies that sub-set of the structures of English, together with the relevant specialised vocabulary, for the domain under question. Like PLANES, LIFER is based on a semantic grammar, but adopts a 'sentence template' approach rather than a 'concept Case frame' one.

The person responsible for building the Q/A system specifies the sub-language in the form of rewrite rules (see section 1.2), which are automatically transformed by LIFER into simplified augmented transition networks. The parser uses these networks to interpret input sentences and to map them onto the appropriate data base query routines.

A simplified user-supplied grammar for the purposes of illustration is the following:

```
S -> <present> the <attribute> of <ship>
present -> what is ¡ [can you] tell me
attribute -> length ¡ beam ¡ class ¡ hull number
ship -> the <shipname>¡<classname> class ship
shipname -> john f. kennedy ¡ constellation ¡ nautilus
classname -> kitty hawk ¡ lafayette
```

The above grammar would account for sentences such as:

```
1 What is the length of Lafayette class ships?
2 What is the hull number of the Nautilus?
3 Can you tell me the class of the John F. Kennedy?
```

Here, actual words are matched as is. The items enclosed in angle brackets are termed 'meta-symbols', which can be matched in several ways, for example:

```
1 as a set (<shipname>= { Constellation, Nautilus, ... } );
```

2 as a predicate applied to carry out a certain test on some string
(e.g. to test whether a string constitutes a date);
3 as the entry node to another transition network.

Note that several tough problems faced by Q/A systems are easily
handled by LIFER, such as certain kinds of spelling mistakes and
ellipsis. For example, if query 2 above contained a mis-spelling such
as 'hull nubmer', this can be quickly detected as the system need only
check in the list of attributes, since only an attribute is accepted
at this point in the query by the grammar. Thus, heavy processing of
substantial amounts of candidate matches is prevented. In a similar
vein, ellipsis can be dealt with in a motivated manner. Thus the
system will achieve the correct interpretation for the following
sequence

Can you tell me the hull number of the Nautilus?
The beam?

as the grammar specifies that 'hull number' and 'beam' belong to the
same class, therefore the reading 'hull number of the beam' is not
considered, but the correct reading 'the beam of the Nautilus' is
recognised.

The most interesting aspect of LIFER is undoubtedly the interface
builder, that is, the suite of interactive tools enabling a user to
specify and construct their own NL interface. It is said of LIFER
that many applications demand only a few days or weeks of work. One of
the most complex applications developed using this system was the
LADDER system which took only a few man-months to develop. LADDER
gives access to a large, geographically widely distributed data base
in the USA, dealing with command and control information for the US
Navy. In this case, the LIFER-produced Q/A interface analyses user
input and produces a general data base query statement, which LADDER
then converts into an actual data base query for a particular data
base of the network.

The interactive tools allow construction and testing of grammatical
patterns, the establishing of word classes and their associated
members, the establishing of fixed phrases, and the declaration of
predicates for the actual data base queries. The end user has access
to some interesting features, notably the paraphrase facility, which
allows one to define new patterns in terms of old ones, while in the
midst of a query session. For example, the user can say

Let 'Describe the Nautilus' be a paraphrase of 'Print
the displacement, hull number and home port of the
Nautilus'.

As far as disadvantages go, LIFER suffers from the same problem as
PLANES: contextual information is not available. Further, the system
cannot deal well with relative clauses or long-distance dependencies
between elements of a sentence. Having said this, it must however be

remembered that LIFER-generated interfaces are not meant to deal with complex sentences, it being a characteristic of special languages that complex sentences are relatively rare.

Perhaps the greatest drawback of the system is that the particular parsing scheme used means that many syntactic generalities cannot be expressed, e.g. a rule written to allow concatenation of similar meta-symbols (e.g. a list of attributes) does not generalise to other categories of meta-symbol, so the builder must explicitly and exhaustively write separate concatenation rules for each meta-symbol, rendering the eventual grammar much bigger.

Nevertheless, LIFER represents a significant system in the Q/A paradigm, in that it stresses the provision of a habitable environment for the interface builder, and allows the naive user to add certain extensions when running the finished system. What probably remains true, though, is that best results are to be achieved by having a linguistic expert, or at least someone conversant with the sub-language, construct the application rules, rather than a linguistically naive person.

5.4.3 INTELLECT

Originally called the ROBOT system, INTELLECT is one of the first commercially available Q/A systems. As opposed to the philosophy of PLANES and LIFER, it operates by generating all possible syntactic interpretations of a sentence, then filtering out those that are semantically impossible. In order to distinguish the semantically plausible from the implausible, the system uses directly the information stored in the data base, about objects and the relations between them. This implies that the data base must be of a particular form. INTELLECT demands no special dictionary, coming provided with merely a general language dictionary. Incorporated in the system is a facility for building inverted files of data object names. This technique gives an extended dictionary capability when activated, yielding, for each data object name, a list of the data domains in which the name occurs. Ambiguity resulting from the detection of a data object name in the input with no helpful context is dealt with pragmatically by simply generating as many data base queries as there are interpretations, then choosing as the correct interpretation the (usually one) query which returns with some hits. To exemplify, a request for 'GREEN FORDS' is on the surface four-ways ambiguous (green – colour; Green – name; Ford – name; Ford – automobile company) but the correct interpretation is achieved in terms of the data base itself, which contains relevant references only to car manufacturers called Ford and to cars coloured green.

As would be expected of a commercially available system, portability and adaptability are seen as important. The inverted file facility ensures that specialised 'dictionaries' can be generated from users' own data base files. It apparently takes about one week to adapt INTELLECT to a new environment.

5.5 MULTILINGUAL NATURAL LANGUAGE INTERFACES

Throughout this chapter, we have been concerned purely with monolingual systems, and have made no reference to the multilingual aspect of NL interfaces. We make no apology for this. There are no multilingual interfaces of an interesting kind extant. All that is available are some data base query languages whose commands are made available in several languages, but these are in fact as limited as a monolingual data base query language, and are rather to be compared to implementations of programming language compilers which accept programs written using foreign language substitutes for the reserved words (e.g. SI .. ALORS for IF .. THEN). What we hope has been made clear in the course of our discussion is that there are many major problems of a basic monolingual (or rather language independent) nature to be overcome in the design of NL interfaces, and that therefore multilingual applications will inevitably take second place, unless there are intrinsic reasons for their development, such as in computer assisted learning (CAL) systems for foreign language teaching. Given the present lack of a general knowledge representation, and of the predominance of English, it is highly likely that it would be a major undertaking to install more than one advanced NL interface to a data base. The relevant research is only likely to be funded by cooperative ventures such as the ESPRIT initiative of the Commission of the European Communities. It could be argued with some justification that multilingual NL interfaces are in fact dependent on advances in machine translation (MT).

However, it seems to us a crude, short-term solution to propose that queries and responses be translated from one language into another, which is then the input to the NL interface proper. If conceived as a long-term solution, this implies a level of MT which demands a high degree of understanding, otherwise much information will necessarily be lost in going from one language into another before formulating data base queries, and most importantly, it will be that information which is most language-bound (focus, discourse phenomena, user beliefs expressed through the user's language, etc.) which will be lost, given current MT techniques. Remember that current MT philosophy is sentence-bound, and furthermore states that one should only analyse as deeply as necessary to achieve an adequate translation (see section 4.4.1), and that this currently does not imply any great degree of understanding of a text by an MT system. Further, output of responses that have undergone MT (such as in retrieval of abstracts as opposed to facts) is likely to cause problems for users, given the state of the art in abstract translation. There is an immediate negative psychological impact on receipt of a translation, even if it is, say, 75 per cent intelligible. This is due to users of IR systems not being used to seeing 'bad' output. If an IR system misses out on some relevant documents, they simply do not appear in the output. That is, the end-user is not normally in a position to evaluate the performance of an IR system, in the same way that an end-user of a MT system is: even ignoring the source text, one can tell whether a translation is intelligible or not. Of interest in this context would be interlingual systems, such as TITUS or the various systems based on Schank's Conceptual Dependency (CD) model. However, these suffer from inherent limitations, and neither TITUS nor CD could be said to have general large-scale implementation possibilities.

The foregoing sounds rather pessimistic as far as multilingual NL interfaces are concerned. However, we must ask ourselves: multilingual interfaces for whom, and for what purpose? Realistically, the bulk of NL interface research emanates from the USA, and is therefore biased towards the treatment of English. English is the major language of the scientific and technological community, with French and German coming poor seconds. Only in Europe, or in officially bilingual states such as Canada, will there be any motivation to provide multilingual NL interfaces, and this motivation will mostly derive from political requirements. It will probably be a long time before there is enough commercial pressure for internationally accessible data bases to provide multilingual access through NL interfaces. An interesting point is made by Dubois, who states that:

> Most information centres of sufficient sophistication to require access to large internationally available data bases are likely to have at least one information scientist with sufficient knowledge of English to carry out searches. This is particularly the case where a controlled vocabulary is available since such a vocabulary is in any case semantically distinct from natural language, and ... the learning of an indexing language whose descriptors are taken from a different natural language to that of the searcher can simply be seen as an extension of the information scientist's normal search skills. (Dubois, 1979, p.6)

In other words, there would have to be powerful reasons for the development and adoption of multilingual interfaces to conventional IR systems.

Indeed, a logically prior step is the development, implementation and proliferation of large-scale knowledge bases, as opposed to the currently numerous conventional data bases available via information networks, most of which are bibliographic data bases. Despite the interest among users for multilingual access to data bases containing factual information, it is unfortunately the case that knowledge engineering techniques are not yet capable of generating such large-scale data bases.

There are therefore four major obstacles to the development of multilingual access to intelligent data bases: first, the lack of sound, general-purpose (or customisable) knowledge representation techniques; second, the fact that discourse analysis techniques are still in an early stage of development; third, the problem of portability of NL interfaces; and last, the lack of knowledge regarding MT in a discourse-oriented, fast data base access environment. As stated above, the problem of generating efficient large-scale knowledge bases could be solved by adopting the ideas set forth by Mylopoulos. With a solid data base foundation, NL interfaces could be more easily elaborated, and a greater degree of portability assured. This is but one possible view of how better NL interfaces could be built. However, it is unlikely that agreement can be reached on a standard method of recording knowledge. In short, there will be many kinds of data base, each specialised towards a different subject and application, many kinds of users, with differing needs, many kinds of special language (sub-language) to be catered for, and so on. The potential diversity of data bases and corresponding NL interfaces is astonishing. It would seem then that we are to be defeated by this diversity, and that we cannot foresee any general NL interface being developed.

5.6 FUTURE TRENDS

However, we believe that future prospects are not so pessimistic, at least not for monolingual NL interfaces. To see why we believe this, let us try to draw together a few points made throughout the chapter, which we repeat here for the sake of convenience, and some other points which we see as important:

1 There is now a better understanding of the relationship between conventional data bases and intelligent knowledge bases. In particular, proposals have been put forward as to how AI techniques could be used to design tools encapsulating the knowledge of designers of conventional and intelligent data bases, which could then be used in the construction of data bases.

2 One of the most attractive features of the LIFER system is its suite of interactive tools designed to aid the specification of a sublanguage for a particular data base application.

3 The INTELLECT system, although restricted to data bases of a certain type, can determine the semantic plausibility of a parse by referring to the data base itself to discover information regarding objects and the relations between them. Further, the dictionary for the system can be extended by processing the data base to extract data object names.

4 There is much interest in AI in the field of automatic programming.

5 Much work has been done in computer science concerning both compiler-compilers, i.e. systems that accept a definition of a programming language and produce a compiler for that language (e.g. Yacc, which is a particularly good example of the genre) and lexical analyser generators. Lexical analysis is typically the first stage of the compilation process when individual words are isolated and recognised as reserved words, user defined variable names, etc. A well-known lexical analyser generator is Lex, which accepts definitions in the form of regular expressions (that is, a language capable of recognising just the sequences possible in character strings).

6 Recent trends in computer science, and especially in software engineering, are towards what is known as rapid prototyping. This involves the realisation that a priori problem solutions are invariably ill-defined, and that it is preferable to refine a sequence of prototypes over an extended time-period, which can serve to validate the problem statement. Moreover, the conventional top-down decomposition of a problem statement into interacting modules (see sction 1.4) has also been seriously called into

question, and cogent arguments made for the adoption of what is called the operational approach to software development. We do not wish to get involved in a detailed discussion of this approach; however, some understanding is necessary of this evolution in computer science, as there are important consequences for work in CL and AI.

The emphasis of the operational approach is on the high-level, formal description of system specifications. The designer uses tools (formal languages) which are based on structures specific to the problem domain being addressed, and hence are totally divorced from questions of implementation. That is, specifications are developed in terms of the problem domain, not in terms of an eventual machine, compiler, or other low-level structure. Crucially, the high-level definition of the problem solution is preserved in behavioural terms, via a series of transformations towards an eventual implementation. This is in direct contrast to the conventional approach, which is more oriented towards forcing a problem solution into an implementational straitjacket, hence inevitably losing many desirable behavioural characteristics.

From our vantage point of observer of all these events and developments in various disciplines, we can note the following concerns that seem to be common to all, to a greater or lesser degree:

1 problem-orientedness
2 formal, high-level specifications
3 implementation independence
4 modifiability and portability
5 (suites of) system-building tools
6 prototyping.

Going further, we can detect a trend towards developing not implementations of individual systems, but rather generators of systems, which ideally generate a class of systems in some problem domain.

What does this imply for the development of future NL interfaces? It seems to us that we must recognise that for the conceivable future, NL interfaces, specifically Q/A systems, will only be able to deal satisfactorily with sub-languages and microworlds. Taking this as our starting point, we then ask how we can best develop interfaces. The traditional answer has been to construct a skeletal system that is then adapted to particular needs. This approach has met with moderate success, although there are many disadvantages, as we have seen, and really many such systems are constrained to a small class of conventional data base types. With our new perspective on trends in various related disciplines, we can propose a different approach, namely to establish an NL interface generation environment, whose tools will accept problem-oriented definitions concerning a class of NL interfaces. Thus it will be possible to have generators for suitable data bases, suitable sub-languages, dictionaries, etc. There is obviously an enormous amount of work to be done here, as we are talking about integrating knowledge from several domains, and in many cases, knowledge that is not fully developed. However, it is not inconceivable that a major project be started, following a rapid prototyping, operational specification methodology, that would lead rapidly to the development of the knowledge required for a general-purpose NL interface generator.

The above proposal may sound idealistic. However, it appears to us to be the only really viable solution to the problem of constructing NL interfaces to the complex knowledge bases of the future. Furthermore, it is not a fanciful proposal; rather, it is founded on techniques and methodologies that are currently receiving much attention in related fields. Moreover, as the problems of monolingual NL interface construction are difficult enough, it is more than likely that multilingual NL interfaces will demand a substantially greater effort, if we proceed as at present. With the proper generation environment, we foresee that the construction of multilingual interfaces will be greatly aided. Note that in the preceding paragraph we included a data base generator in our generation environment. Why would we want to do this, when we are talking of interfaces to data bases, which presumably already exist?

Our reason is twofold: first, there is a lot to be said for an expert tool to enable the construction of efficient knowledge bases; second, we firmly believe that the only acceptable way to interact with knowledge bases is via natural language, hence it would be inconceivable to generate a data base without at the same time generating a NL interface for it - that is, data base and NL interface will go hand-in-hand. In other words, the generation environment we have specified in general terms recognises that NL interfaces are an integral part of knowledge bases, so what we have in fact specified is a generation environment not so much for NL interfaces, but for knowledge bases which include a NL interface as part and parcel of their design. As our subject was NL interfaces, we discussed their elaboration from the point of view of grafting an interface onto a data base. We are now in a position to revise our ideas concerning interfaces, and to realize that, although there will continue to be a market for interfaces to existing data bases, increasingly data bases will be developed along with an NL interface. This is not to say that the NL interface will be totally and inextricably bound to the knowledge base, as with present integrated systems. Rather, the binding will be carried out in a motivated fashion by means of a generator, and this by no means precludes the existence of one general specification of an interface (among many others) for a certain class of data base (among other classes) whose definition can be tuned for a particular purpose. The reader must be careful to distinguish here between a general specification for an NL interface which can be modified and then input to a generator, and a skeletal interface, elements of which can be augmented. The latter is a much more restricted device, as there is an already existing framework. The former represents an incomplete specification which can be augmented, but presupposes no existing framework. What does preexist is the metaknowledge within the generator concerning a wide class of NL interfaces.

5.7 CONCLUSION

At present, there exist many IR systems which go some way towards satisfying information needs. However, as we have seen, these are rather limited, and are inherently imprecise in terms of the answers (sets of documents) that they give, in that end users are expected to analyse (hopefully) relevant documents to discover (perhaps) the information they seek. For various reasons, CL techniques have not been adopted in these systems. On the other hand, numerous Q/A systems have been developed over the years. These, however, remain for the most part small scale systems which are unable to handle vast quantities of data, and they are moreover constrained in terms of domain of application (a microworld) and, invariably, of the size of the subset of language they can handle. There are many severe problems facing the designer of a Q/A system. However, those systems that are operational can achieve modest results, which we can summarise as follows:

1 Adequate interrogation of small, limited domain data bases, using a reasonably wide subset of language. Better results achieved by subject specialists than by naive users.
2 Simple responses to direct questions.
3 Basic capability to handle simple pronominal reference and some types of ellipsis.
4 Spelling correction as simple aid to robust processing.
5 Avoidance of several major classes of problem by use of semantic grammars (however, semantic grammars remain manageable only at the level of small, restricted systems).

In many ways, mainstream CL has been of little help, given its concentration on sentence rather than discourse linguistics. Thus, it is only now that advances are beginning to be made in modelling user beliefs, determining dialogue focus, resolving ambiguity between literal and indirect interpretations and providing extended responses. Looking to the future, major advances are only likely if there is closer contact between IR system designers and Q/A system designers, and if the portability barrier for Q/A systems can be successfully overcome.

For successful NL interfaces to be built to interface with other kinds of data base systems, e.g. structured (non-conventional) data bases, (intelligent) knowledge bases, expert systems, etc. much research needs to be done, and substantial advances will probably not be made until these relatively new kinds of data base have reached the same level of stability as conventional data bases. By this we mean that there is no one generally acceptable or adequate model for the representation of knowledge, whereas conventional data bases are implemented according to one of the three well-understood models (hierarchical, network and - increasingly - relational). The views of Mylopoulos (1983) on the potential relationship between conventional data bases and knowledge bases seem to us to point to a fruitful future for Q/A systems, if the tools can be developed to generate, upon input of precise high-level definitions, efficiently implemented intelligent data bases. Here especially then we can appreciate how the combination of CL, AI, IR and data base design theory can help us to develop intelligent NL interfaces that will provide a Q/A capability for a wide class of domain-specific applications.

We trust we have given the reader a useful insight into the problems of constructing NL interfaces, and into the various solutions to these that have been adopted or proposed. Much of our discussion has been based on monolingual aspects, but we hope that it is clear that in the light of the difficulties encountered in the monolingual sphere, we cannot yet expect great advances in the multilingual one. What we have been concerned to do, however, is to highlight the problems in the general area, to illustrate via reference to existing interesting systems, and to point to a possible productive direction which could prove beneficial both for the elaboration of models of NL interfaces and for their construction.

5.8 FURTHER READING

(The field of question-answering is a relatively new one. Moreover, we were concerned to give the reader an appreciation of current issues, as it is only recently that the most interesting problems have been addressed. As a consequence, we can cite few major publications in the form of books which discuss these issues. The majority of publications which follow are hence articles in scientific journals.)

IR systems
A standard reference work is Salton and McGill (1983). The following concentrate on the relationship between IR and linguistics or CL: Montgomery (1972), Sparck Jones and Kay (1972), Walker et al. (1977) and Walker (1981). The objectives of indexing are set out in Keen (1977). Document analysis, automatic keyword extracting and automatic indexing are discussed by Sparck Jones (1971), Salton (1970, 1971) and Sparck Jones and Kay (1972). Judgements of results from IR can be found in Sparck Jones and Kay (1972), Walker et al. (1977), van Rijsbergen (1979) and Salton and McGill (1983). Criticism of the theoretical foundations of IR is given by Walker (1981). An early prediction of libraries and information systems of the future can be found in Licklider (1965).

Q/A systems
General introductory works include Waltz (1977), Rahmstorf and Ferguson (1978), Bolc (1980), Tennant (1981), Kaplan (1982), J. King (1983) and Hayes and Carbonell (1983). Those readers interested in the earlier systems are advised to consult Simmons (1970), Waltz (1977) and Barr and Feigenbaum (1982). LUNAR is described in Woods et al. (1972), which also contains a discussion of the difference between expert and non-expert users. TEAM is discussed by Grosz (1983). The distinction between integrated and front end systems is discussed by Karlgren (1977). The idea of modelling users' beliefs, and investigation into the role of mutually held knowledge and beliefs is reported in Joshi (1982) and Nadathur and Joshi (1983). Lehnert (1980) talks about the difference between the worlds of AI and IR.

Regarding types of knowledge, see Hayes and Carbonell (1983) for a general tutorial discussion. On knowledge of focus, see Grosz (1981) and Sidner (1979, 1983). Linguistic knowledge is discussed by Tennant (1981). Interest in Speech Acts stems from Searle (1969). The treatment of deviant output is discussed in Kwasny and Sondheimer

(1979, 1981), Weischedel and Black (1980) and Hayes and Reddy (1983).
On generating output, see Webber (1983).

Current research into incorrect presuppositions is reported in
Webber and Mays (1983) and Kaplan (1979, 1981). On monitoring as
response, see Webber et al. (1983). 'Discontinuities' are discussed by
Siklossy (1978). Webber and Joshi (1982) discuss the need for systems
to explain their responses. Anticipation of further questions is a
feature of IMP (Jameson, 1983), and HAM-ANS (Wahlster et al., 1983).
The term 'extended response' is from Cohen et al. (1982).

Conventional data bases and knowledge bases
The typology of Q/A systems is from Karlgren (1977). Ullman (1980)
discusses conventional data bases at length. The relationship between
data bases and knowledge bases is investigated by Brodie and Zilles
(1981) (particularly the article by Mylopoulus, 1981), Brodie et al.
(1983) (and particularly the article by Mylopoulos and Levesque, 1983)
and Mylopoulos (1983). Expert systems are discussed informally in
Feigenbaum and McCorduck (1984), and in more detail in Hayes-Roth and
Lenert (1984), Buchanan and Shortliffe (1984), Stefik et al. (1982)
and Lauriere (1982).

Examples
For PLANES, see Waltz (1978). Somers (1985) discusses this system from
the point of view of Case Grammar, while Tennant (1981) gives a more
general discussion. JETS is described in Finin et al. (1979).

LIFER is described in Hendrix (1977a,b). LADDER is presented in
Hendrix et al. (1978). Recent work on constructing interactive tools
is reported in Hendrix and Lewis (1981), which deals with the use of
interactive dialogues with data base administrators to create new
interfaces.

INTELLECT is discussed by Harris (1977a, 1977b, 1979).

Multilingual NL interfaces
For CAL in general, see Barr and Feigenbaum (1982) or Sleeman and
Brown (in press). Further references to CAL may be found in section
1.6. The negative psychological reaction to translated output is
suggested in Dubois (1979), which also deals with multilingual
information systems from an information scientist's point of view. See
Tedd (1979), Barnes (1983) and Ananiadou (1985) for descriptions of
TITUS. There are numerous references to Schank's work: Barr and
Feigenbaum (1981) provide a brief description, while Schank and
Abelson (1977) have more detail.

Future trends
On automatic programming, see Barr and Feigenbaum (1982), Biermann
(1976) or Hammer and Ruth (1979), while Heidorn (1976) discusses
automatic programming from NL. Compiler-compilers and lexical
analysers are discussed in Aho and Ullman (1977). Yacc is described in
Johnson (1975), and Lex in Lesk (1975). 'Rapid prototyping' is
presented in Giddings (1984), and the operational approach is
discussed by Zave (1984). Johnson et al. (1984) discuss the
application of a rapid prototyping, operational approach to the
development of software for the EUROTRA MT project.

Bibliography

AFNOR (ed.) (1973), Etude de l'enregistrement et du traitement automatique du vocabulaire normalisé a l'AFNOR. ISO/INFCO 115.

AFNOR (ed.) (1975), 'La banque automatisée de données terminologiques de l'AFNOR, NORMATERM', Courrier de la Normalisation no. 245 (Sept.-Oct. 1975), Paris, AFNOR.

AFTERM (1976), Terminologies 76, Paris, La maison du dictionnaire.

AFTERM (ed.) (1978), Etude de faisabilité d'une banque de données terminologiques (documents contributifs), Paris, AFTERM.

Aho, A.V., Hopcroft, J.E. and Ullman, J.D. (1974), The Design and Analysis of Computer Algorithms, Reading, Mass., Addison-Wesley.

Aho, A.V. and Ullman, J.D. (1972), Principles of Compiler Design, Reading, Mass., Addison-Wesley.

Akmajian, A. and Heny, F. (1975), An Introduction to the Principles of Transformational Syntax, Cambridge, Mass., MIT Press.

Allerton, D. (1979), Essentials of Grammatical Theory, London, Routledge and Kegan Paul.

Al-Kasimi, A.M. (1983), 'The interlingual/translation dictionary'. In Hartmann (1983a), pp.153-162.

ALPAC (Automatic Language Processing Advisory Committee) (1966), Language and Machines, Computers in Translation and Linguistics, Washington DC, Division of Behavioral Sciences, National Academy of Sciences, National Research Council.

Ananiadou, S. (1985), 'A brief survey of some current operational systems'. In King (1985b).

Anderson, J. and Kline, P. (1979), 'A learning system and its psychological implications', Proceedings of IJCAI 1979, pp.16-21.

Arnold, D. and Johnson, R. (1984), 'Robust processing in machine translation'. In COLING 1984, pp.472-475.

ARPA SUR Steering Committee (1977), 'Speech understanding systems: Report of a steering committee', Artificial Intelligence, vol. 9, pp.307-316.

Bakulina, I.I. (ed.) (1979), Essential Problems in Terminology for Informatics and Documentation (FID 569), Moscow, All-Union Institute of Scientific and Technical Information.

Bar-Hillel, Y. (1960), 'The present status of automatic translation of languages', Advances in Computers, vol. 1, pp.91-163.

Bar-Hillel, Y. (1971), 'Some reflections on the present outlook for high-quality machine translation'. In Lehmann, W.P. and Stachowitz, R. (eds.), Feasibility study on fully automatic high quality translation, volume 1, New York, Griffiss Air Force Base, Rome Air Development Center, pp.73-76.

Barnes, A.M.N. (1983), An investigation into the syntactic structures of abstracts, and the feasibility of an Interlingua for their translation by machine, Manchester, Centre for Computational Linguistics, UMIST, CCL/UMIST report no. 83/4.

Barr, A. and Feigenbaum, E.A. (eds) (1981), The Handbook of Artificial Intelligence, vol. 1., London, Pitman.

Barr, A. and Feigenbaum, E.A. (eds) (1982), The Handbook of Artificial Intelligence,. vol. 2., London, Pitman.

Becker, J.D. (1984), 'Multilingual word processing', Scientific American, vol. 251, July, pp.82-93.

Bejoint, H. (1981), 'The foreign student's use of monolingual English dictionaries: a study of language needs and reference skills', Applied Linguistics, vol. 2, pp.207-222.

Berner, K.E. (1976), 'Le système d'information lexicographique LEXIS de l'office fédéral des langues'. In AFTERM (1976).

Berwick, R. and Weinberg, A. (1984), The Grammatical Basis of Linguistic Performance, Cambridge, Mass., MIT Press.

de Bessé, B. (1976), 'L'Association française de terminologie'. In AFTERM (1976).

de Bessé, B. (1978), 'Les activités terminologiques de la société Siemens'. In AFTERM (1978).

de Bessé, B. (1979), 'AFTERM 79', Courrier de la Normalisation 265.

de Bessé, B. and Mosler, A-M. (eds.) (1985), Analyse des Moyens à mettre en oeuvre pour rassembler l'ensemble des terminologies multi-lingues existant en Europe et pour créer une banque des données accessible à tous - Etude EUROTERM. Agence Linguistique Européenne (report submitted to CEC).

Biermann, A.W. (1976), 'Approaches to automatic programming'. In Rubinoff and Yovits (1976).

Boden, M. (1977), Artificial Intelligence and Natural Man, Brighton, Harvester.

Bolc, L. (ed.) (1980), Natural Language Question-Answering Systems, London, Hanser-Verlag and Macmillan Press.

Bresnan, J. (ed.) (1982), The Mental Representation of Grammatical Relations, Cambridge, Mass., MIT Press.

Brinkmann, K.H. (1975), 'The TEAM Program System', Philips Terminology Bulletin, vol. 4, nos. 2/3, Eindhoven, Philips.

Brinkmann, K.H. (1979), 'Use of the TEAM Terminology Data Bank for the terminology work of DIN', Proceedings of the International Symposium on Theoretical and Methodological Problems of Terminology, Moscow.

Brodie, M. and Zilles, S. (eds) (1981), 'Data Abstraction, Databases and Conceptual Modelling', SIGART Newsletter, January 1981.

Brodie, M.L., Mylopoulos, J. and Schmidt, J.V. (eds) (1983), On Conceptual Modelling, New York,Springer-Verlag.

Brunold, H.P. (1976) 'Le système TEAM'. In AFTERM (1976).

Buchanan, B.G. and Shortliffe, E.H. (1984), Rule-based Expert Systems, Reading, Mass., Addison-Wesley.

Burton, R.R. and Brown, J.S. (1979), 'Toward a natural-language capability for computer-assisted instruction'. In O'Neill (1979).

Carbonell, J.R. (1970), 'AI in CAI: an artificial intelligence approach to computer-assisted instruction', IEEE Transactions on Man-machine Systems, vol. 11, pp.190-202.

Carbonell, J., Cullingford, R.E. and Gershman. A.V. (1978), Knowledge-based Machine Translation, Research Report no. 146, Department of Computer Science, Yale University, New Haven CT.

CEC (Commission of the European Communities) (1977), Overcoming the Language Barrier, München, Verlag Dokumentation, 2 vols.

Cerri, S.A. and Merger, M.-F. (1983), 'Learning translation skills with a knowledge-based tutor: French-Italian conjunctions in context', Proceedings of the First Conference of the European Chapter of the Association for Computational Linguistics, pp.133-138.

Chandioux, J. and Gueraud, M.-F. (1981), 'Météo: un système à l'épreuve du temps'. In Kittredge (1981a), pp.18-22.

Chauche, J. (1975), 'The ATEF and CETA system', American Journal of Computational Linguistics, microfiche 17, pp.21-39.

Chevalier, M., Isabelle, P., Labelle, F. and Lainé, C. (1981), 'La traductologie appliquée a la traduction automatique'. In Kittredge (1981a), pp.35-47.

Chomsky, N. (1963) 'Formal properties of grammars'. In Luce, R.D., Bush, R.R. and Galanter, E. (eds), Handbook of Mathematical Psychology, volume 2, New York, Wiley, pp.323-418.

Clerc, M.-G. (1980), 'Le centre de documentation de l'AFNOR et la diffusion de l'information terminologique normalisée', META, vol. 25, pt. 1.

Clerc, M.-G. and Laurent, J. (1976), 'NORMATERM, la banque de données terminologiques normalisées de l'AFNOR'. In AFTERM (1976).

Clocksin, W.F. and Mellish, C.S. (1981), Programming in Prolog, Berlin, Springer-Verlag.

Cohen, P.R., Perrault, C.R. and Allen, J.F. (1982), 'Beyond question-answering'. In Lehnert and Ringle (eds) (1982).

COLING (1980), COLING 80: Proceedings of the 8th International Conference on Computational Linguistics, Tokyo.

COLING (1984), 10th International Conference on Computational Linguistics - 22nd Annual Meeting of the Association for Computational Linguistics (Proceedings of Coling84, Stanford University, California).

Colmerauer, A. (1971), Les systèmes-Q, ou un formalisme pour analyser et synthétiser des phrases sur ordinateur, Publ. int. no. 43, Projet de Traduction Automatique, Université de Montréal.

Cowie, A.P. (1983a), 'On specifying grammar'. In Hartmann (1983a), pp.99-107.

Cowie, A.P. (1983b), 'The pedagogical/learner's dictionary: English dictionaries for the foreign learner'. In Hartmann (1983a), pp.135-144.

Cowie, A.P. (1984), 'EFL Dictionaries: past achievements and present needs'. In Hartmann (1984), pp.155-164.

Crystal, D. (1980), A First Dictionary of Linguistics and Phonetics, London, Deutsch.

Dahl, O.J., Dijkstra, E.W. and Hoare, C.A.R. (1972), Structured Programming, New York, Academic Press.

Damerau, F.J. (1978), 'The derivation of answers from logical forms in a question answering system', American Journal of Computational Linguistics, Microfiche 75, pp.3-42.

DANTERM (DANTERM Project Group) (1979), 'DANTERM - the Danish Terminological Data Bank', CEBAL, no. 5. Copenhagen, Nyt Nordisk Farlag Arnold Busck.

Davis, R. and King, J. (1977), 'An overview of Production Systems'. In Elcock, E.W. and Michie, D. (eds), Machine Intelligence 8: Machine Representation of Knowledge, Chichester, Ellis Horwood, pp.300-332.

Dubois, C.P.R. (1979), 'Multilingual information systems: some criteria for the choice of specific techniques', Journal of Information Science, vol. 1, pp.5-12.

Dubuc, R. (1972), 'A description of the TERMIUM System of the Bank of Terminology', META, vol. 17, Montreal.

Dubuc, R. (1975), Description du systeme TERMIUM, Montreal, Banque de Terminologie, Univ. de Montréal.

Ducrot, J.-M. (1974), 'Perspectives et avantages offerts par la traduction automatique des analyses de documents selon la méthode TITUS', 1er Congres national francais sur l'information et la documentation, Communications, Paris.

Elliston, J.S.G. (1979), 'Computer-aided translation, a business viewpoint'. In Snell (1979), pp.149-158.

Farrington, B. (1984), The Scottish Computer-Based French Learning Project. Progress Report, University of Aberdeen Language Laboratories, Aberdeen.

Feigenbaum, E.A. and McCorduck, P. (1984), The Fifth Generation, London, Pan Books.

Felber, H. et al. (eds) (1979), Terminologie als angewandte Sprachwissenschaft, Munich, Saur.

Finin, T., Goodman, B. and Tennant, H. (1979), 'JETS: Achieving completeness through coverage and closure', Proceedings of IJCAI 1979, pp.275-281.

Fortin, J.M. (1974), La banque de terminologie du Québec, Québec, Banque de Terminologie.

Fortin, J.M. and Lebel-Harou, L. (1976), 'Traitement automatique des données terminologiques, rapport spécifique de la BTQ a cette perspective'. In AFTERM (1976).

François, P. (1976), 'EURODICAUTOM: le résultat d'un travail pluri-disciplinaire'. In AFTERM (1976).

Frandsen, L. and Nistrup, B. (1979), 'Setting up and operation of the Danish Terminological Data Bank'. In Hanon and Pedersen (1979).

Garvin, P.L. (1972), On Machine Translation: Selected Papers, The Hague, Mouton.

Garvin, P.L. (1976), 'Machine translation in the seventies'. In F. Papp and G. Szepe, (eds.), Papers in Computational Linguistics, The Hague, Mouton, pp.445-459.

Gazdar, G., Klein, E., Pullum, G. and Sag, I. (1985), Generalized Phrase Structure Grammar, Oxford, Blackwell.

Georgeff, M. (1982), 'Procedural control in production systems', Artificial Intelligence, vol. 18, pp.175-201.

Giddings, R.V. (1984), 'Accommodating uncertainty in software design', Communications of the ACM, vol. 27, pp.428-434.

Goetschalckx, J. (1977), 'Terminological activities in the European institutions, with special reference to EURODICAUTOM'. In CEC (1977).

Goetschalckx, J. and Rolling, L. (1982), Lexicography in the Electronic Age, Amsterdam, North-Holland.

Grosz, B. (1977), The representation and use of focus in dialogue understanding, TR-151, SRI International, Menlo Park, Cal.

Grosz, B.J. (1981), 'Focusing and description in natural language dialogues'. In Joshi et al. (1981).

Grosz, B.J. (1983), 'TEAM: A transportable natural language interface system', Proceedings of the Conference on Applied Natural Language Processing, pp.39-45. Association for Computational Linguistics.

Hall, P.A.V. (1975), Computational Structures: an Introduction to Non-numeric Computing, London, Macdonald & Jane's.

Hammer, M. and Ruth, G. (1979), 'Automating the software development process'. In Wegner (1979).

Hanon, S. and Pedersen, V. (eds) (1979), Human Translation - Machine Translation (Noter og Kommentarer 39), Odense, Romansk Institut, Odense University.

Harris, L.R. (1977a), 'ROBOT: A high performance natural language processor for data base query', SIGART Newsletter, no. 61, pp.39-40.

Harris, L.R. (1977b), 'User-oriented data base query with the ROBOT natural language query system', International Journal of Man-Machine Studies, vol. 9, pp.697-713.

Harris, L.R. (1979), 'Experience with ROBOT in 12 commercial natural language data base query applications', Proceedings of IJCAI 1979, pp.365-368.

Hartmann, R.R.K. (ed.) (1979), Dictionaries and their Users: Papers from the 1978 BAAL Seminar on Lexicography, Exeter Linguistic Studies 4, Exeter University.

Hartmann, R.R.K. (ed.) (1983a), Lexicography: Principles and Practice, London, Academic Press.

Hartmann, R.R.K. (1983b), 'The bilingual learner's dictionary and its uses', Multilingua, vol. 2, pp.195-201.

Hartmann, R.R.K. (ed.) (1984), LEXeter '83 Proceedings: Papers from the International Conference on Lexicography at Exeter, 9-12 September 1983, Tubingen, Max Niemeyer Verlag.

Hatherall, G. (1984), 'Studying dictionary use: some findings and proposals'. In Hartmann (1984), pp.183-189.

Hayes, P.J. and Carbonell, J.J. (1983), 'Natural Language Tutorial – IJCAI-83, Supplementary Notes'. In Ritchie and Albers (1983).

Hayes, P.J. and Reddy, D.R. (1983), 'Steps toward graceful interaction in spoken and written man-machine communication', International Journal of Man-Machine Studies, vol. 18, pp.211-284.

Hayes-Roth, F. and Lenat, D.B. (1984), Building Expert Systems, New York, McGraw-Hill.

Heidorn, G.E. (1976), 'Automatic programming through natural language dialogue', IBM Journal of Research and Development, vol. 4, pp. 302-313.

Heidorn, G.E., Jensen, K., Miller, L.A., Byrd, R.J. and Chodorow, M.S. (1982), 'The EPISTLE text critiquing system', IBM Systems Journal, vol. 21, pp.305-326.

Heinisz-Dostert, B., Macdonald, R.R. and Zarechnak, M. (1979), Machine Translation, The Hague, Mouton.

Hendrix, G.G. (1977a), 'LIFER: A natural language interface facility', SIGART Newsletter, no. 61, pp.25-26.

Hendrix, G.G. (1977b), 'Human engineering for applied natural language processing', Proceedings of IJCAI 1977, pp.183-191.

Hendrix, G.G., Sacerdoti, E.D., Sagalowicz, D. and Slocum, J. (1978), 'Developing a natural language interface to complex data', ACM Transactions on Database Systems, vol. 9, pp.105-147.

Hendrix, G.G. and Lewis, W. (1981), 'Transportable natural-language interfaces to databases, Proceedings of 19th Annual Meeting of the Association for Computational Linguistics, pp.159-166.

Hjulstad, H. (1984), 'Terminology work in Norway and the Norwegian Term Bank'. In Hartmann (1984), pp.352-354.

Hobbs, J.R., Walker, D.E. and Amsler, R.A. (1982), 'Natural langauge access to structured text'. In Horecky (1982), pp.127-132.

Hockey, S. and Marriot, I. (1982), Oxford Concordance Program, Oxford University Computing Service.

Hoffmann, E. (1978), 'Maschinelle Übersetzungshilfen im Bundessprachenamt'. In Krallmann (1978).

Horecký, J. (1982) (ed.). COLING 82: Proceedings of the Ninth International Conference on Computational Linguistics, Amsterdam, North-Holland.

Horowitz,E. and Sahni, S. (1976), Fundamentals of Data Structures, London, Pitman.

Hortzwath, D. (1975), TERMIUM ou la banque de terminologie, Montréal, Univ. de Montréal.

Huddleston, R. (1984), Introduction to the Grammar of English, Cambridge, Cambridge University Press.

Hurford, J. and B. Heasley (1983), Semantics: A Coursebook, Cambridge, Cambridge University Press.

Hutchins, W.J. (1978), 'Machine translation and machine-aided translation', Journal of Documentation, vol. 34, pp.119-159.

Hutchins, W.J. (1982), 'The evolution of machine translation systems'. In Lawson (1982), pp.21-36.

Hvalkof, S. (1982), Étude comparative des données terminologiques des banques de terminologie DANTERM, BTQ, EURODICAUTOM, NORMATERM, O.F.L. et SIEMENS, Arhus, Denmark, École des hautes etudes commerciales et des langues modernes de Arhus, Département de français.

INFOTERM (ed.) (1976), INFOTERM Series 3 - First INFOTERM Symposium - International Cooperation in Terminology, Munich, Verlag Dokumentation.

INFOTERM (1980), 'Report on Hispanoterm', INFOTERM Newsletter, no. 17.

Isabelle, P. and Bourbeau, L. (1985), 'TAUM-AVIATION: its technical features and some experimental results', Computational Linguistics, vol. 11, pp. 18-27.

ISO/TC 37/WG 4 (1979), Draft Proposal: Format for Terminological/ Lexicographic Data Interchange on Magnetic Tape (MATER), Paris/ Wien, ISO Committee on Computational Aids in Terminology and Lexicography.

ISO 2709 (1973), Documentation - Formats for bibliographic information interchange on magnetic tape, ISO TC 46.

Jameson, A. (1983), 'Impression monitoring in evaluation-oriented dialogue', Proceedings of IJCAI 1983, pp.616-620.

Johnson, R.L. (1983), 'Parsing - an MT perspective'. In Sparck Jones and Wilks (1983), pp.32-38.

Johnson, R.L., Krauwer, S., Rosner, M. and Varile, N. (1983), 'Controlling complex systems of linguistic rules', American Journal of Computational Linguistics, vol. 9, pp.199-201.

Johnson, R.L., Krauwer, S., Rosner, M. and Varile, N. (1984), 'The design of the kernel architecture for the Eurotra software', COLING 1984, pp.226-235.

Johnson, S.C. (1975), Yacc: Yet Another Compiler-Compiler, Computing Science Technical Report no. 32, Bell Labs, Murray Hill, N.J.

135

Joshi, A.K. (1982), 'Mutual beliefs in question-answer systems'. In
Smith (1982), pp.181-197.

Joshi, A.K., Webber, B. and Sag, I. (eds) (1981), Elements of
Discourse Understanding, Cambridge, Cambridge University Press.

Josselson, H.H. (1971), 'Automatic translation of languages since
1960: a linguist's view'. In Alt, F.L. and Rubinoff, M. (eds),
Advances in Computers II, New York, Academic Press, pp.1-58.

Kaplan, S.J. (1979), Cooperative responses from a portable natural
language data base query system, Doctoral dissertation, Dept. of
Computer and Information Science, Univ. of Pennsylvania.

Kaplan, S.J. (1981), 'Appropriate responses to inappropriate
questions'. In Joshi (1981).

Kaplan, S.J. (1982), 'Special Section: Natural Language Processing',
SIGART Newsletter, no. 79, pp.27-109 and 80, pp.59-61.

Karlgren, H. (1977), 'Homeosemy: On the linguistics of information
retrieval'. In Walker et al. (1977).

Kay, M. (1973), 'The MIND system'. In Rustin, R. (ed.) Natural
Language Processing, New York, Algorithmics Press, pp.155-188.

Kay, M. (1976), 'Experiments with a powerful parser', American Journal
of Computational Linguistics, microfiche 43.

Keen, E.M. (1977), 'On the generation and searching of entries in
printed subject indexes', Journal of Documentation, vol. 33,
pp.15-45.

King, J. (ed) (1983), Special Issue on AI and Databases. SIGART
Newsletter no. 86.

King, M. (1982), 'Eurotra: an attempt to achieve multilingual MT'. In
Lawson (1982), pp.139-147.

King, M. (ed.) (1983), Parsing Natural Language, London, Academic
Press.

King, M. (1985a), Article in King (1985b).

King, M. (ed.) (1985b), Machine Translation Today, Edinburgh,
Edinburgh University Press.

King, M. and Perschke, S. (1982), 'EUROTRA and its objectives',
Multilingua, vol. 1, pp.27-32.

Kittredge, R. (1981a), (ed.) 'L'informatique au service de la
traduction', META, vol. 26, no. 1.

Kittredge, R. (1981b), 'The development of automated translation
systems in Canada', Lebende Sprachen vol. 26, pp.100-103.

Klatt, D.H. (1977), 'Review of the ARPA speech understanding project', Journal of the Acoustical Society of America, vol. 62, pp.1345-1366.

Knowles, F.E. (1984), 'Dictionaries and computers'. In Hartmann (1984), pp.301-314.

Krallmann, D. (1978), Kolloquium zur Lage der Linguistischen Datenverarbeitung, Essen, LDV-Fittings e.V.

Krollmann, F. (1978), 'User aspects of an automatic aid to translation as employed in a large translation service'. In CEC (1977).

Kwasny, S.C. and Sondheimer, N.K. (1979), 'Ungrammaticality and extragrammaticality in natural language understanding systems', Proceedings of the 17th Meeting of the Association for Computational Linguistics, pp.19-23.

Kwasny, S.C. and Sondheimer, N.K. (1981), 'Relaxation techniques for parsing ill-formed input', American Journal of Computational Linguistics, vol. 7, pp.99-108.

Laberge, D. and Samuels, S. (eds) (1975), Basic Processing in Reading, Perception and Comprehension, Hillsdale, N.J., Lawrence Erlbaum.

Lambrecht, F.H. (1978), Ifugaw-English Dictionary, Baguio City, The Catholic Vicar Apostolic of the Mountain Province.

Landsbergen, J. (1982), 'Machine translation based on logically isomorphic Montague grammars', In Horecký (1982), pp.175-181.

Landsbergen, J. (1985), Article in King (1985b).

Laurent, J. (1976), 'NORMATERM: sa conception, son exploitation et sa place dans le réseau international d'information sur les normes'. In INFOTERM (1976).

Laurent, J. (1977), 'Utilization of the technical terminology standardized at AFNOR'. In CEC (1977).

Lauriere, J.-L. (1982), 'Representation et utilisation des connaissances', Technique et Science Informatiques, vol. 1, pp.25-42 and 109-133.

Lawson, V. (ed.) (1982), Practical Experience of Machine Translation, Amsterdam, North-Holland.

Lawson, V. (1983), 'Machine translation'. In Picken, C. (ed.), Translator's Handbook, London, Aslib, pp.81-88.

Lea, W. (ed.) (1980), Trends in Speech Recognition, Englewood Cliffs, N.J., Prentice-Hall.

Lea, W. and Shoup, J. (1980), 'Specific contributions of the ARPA-SUR project'. In Lea (1980).

Lehnert, W.G. (1980), 'Question answering in natural language processing'. In Bolc (1980).

Lehnert, W.G., Black, J.B., and Reiser, B.J. (1981), 'Summarizing narratives'. Proceedings of IJCAI 1981.

Lehnert, W.G. and Ringle, M.H. (eds) (1982), Strategies for Natural Language Processing, Hillsdale, N.J., Lawrence Erlbaum.

Lesk, M.E. (1975), Lex: a Lexical Analyzer Generator, Computing Science Technical Report no. 39, Bell Labs, Murray Hill, N.J.

Levy, R. (1978a), 'Commission des Communautés Européennes'. In AFTERM (1978).

Levy, R. (1978b), 'Association française de normalisation'. In AFTERM (1978).

Licklider, J.C.R. (1965), Libraries of the Future, Cambridge, Mass., MIT Press.

Locke, W.N. and Booth, A.D. (eds) (1955), Machine Translation of Languages, New York, The Technology Press of the Massachussets Institute of Technology/John Wiley.

Loffler-Laurian, A.-M. (coord) (1984), 'Traduction automatique, aspects européens', Contrastes, hors série A4.

Loh, S-C. (1976), 'Machine translation: past, present, and future', ALLC Bulletin, vol. 4, pp.105-114.

Loh, S-C. and Kong, L. (1977), 'Computer translation of Chinese scientific journals'. In CEC (1977), vol. 1, pp.631-645.

Loh, S-C. and Kong, L. (1979), 'An interactive on-line machine translation system'. In Snell (1979), pp.135-148.

Lurquin, G. (1982), 'The orthophonic dictionary'. In Goetschalckx and Rolling (1982), pp.99-107.

Lyons, J. (1977a), Semantics (2 vols), Cambridge, Cambridge University Press.

Lyons, J. (1977b), Chomsky, London, Fontana/Collins.

Lyons, J. (1981a), Language and Linguistics, Cambridge, Cambridge University Press.

Lyons, J. (1981b), Language, Meaning and Context, London, Fontana.

Lytinen, S.L. and Schank, R.C. (1982), Representation and Translation, Research Report no. 234, Department of Computer Science, Yale University, New Haven, CT.

McNaught, J. (1981), 'Terminological Data Banks: a model for a British Linguistic Data Bank (LDB)', Aslib Proceedings, vol. 33, pp.320-323.

McNaught, J. and Nkwenti Azeh, B. (1983), European Cooperation in Terminological Data Banks, CCL/UMIST Report no. 83/13, Manchester, Centre for Computational Linguistics, UMIST.

Maas, H.-D. (1977), 'The Saarbrücken automatic translation system (SUSY)'. In CEC (1977), vol. 1, pp.585-592.

Maas, H.-D. (1978), 'Das Saarbrücker Übersetzungssystem SUSY'. Sprache und Datenverarbeitung, vol. 1, pp.43-61.

Maas, H.-D. (1985), Article in King (1985b).

Marchuk, Yu.N. (1984), 'Machine translation in the U.S.S.R.', Computers and the Humanities, vol. 18, pp.39-46.

Mays, E., Joshi, A.K. and Webber, B.L. (1982) 'Taking the initiative in natural language date base interactions', Proceedings of ECAI 1982, pp.255-256.

Melby, A. (1981), 'Translators and machines - can they cooperate?'. In Kittredge (1981a), pp.23-34.

Melby, A. (1983), 'Computer-assisted translation systems: the standard design and a multi-level design', Proceedings of the Conference on Applied Natural Language Processing, pp.174-177. Association for Computational Linguistics.

Melby, A. (1985), 'Recipe for a translator work station'. In King (1985b).

Mellish, C. (1983), 'Incremental semantic interpretation in a modular parsing system'. In Sparck Jones and Wilks (1983), pp.148-155.

Merkin, R. (1983), 'The historical/academic dictionary'. In Hartmann (1983a), pp.123-133.

Merkin, R. (1984), 'Historical dictionaries and the computer - another view'. In Hartmann (1984), pp.377-384.

Metzing, D. (ed.) (1979), Frame Conceptions and Text Understanding, Berlin, Walter de Gruyter.

Minsky, M. (1967), Computation: Finite and Infinite Machines, Englewood Cliffs, N.J., Prentice Hall.

Montgomery, C.A. (1972), 'Linguistics and information science', Journal of the American Society for Information Science, pp.195-219.

Moulin, A. (1983), 'LSP dictionaries for EFL learners'. In Hartmann (1983a), pp.144-152.

Mylopoulos, J. (1981), 'A perspective for research on conceptual modelling'. In Brodie and Zilles (1981).

Mylopoulos, J. (1983), 'Knowledge representation and databases', Proceedings of IJCAI 1983, pp.1202-1204.

Mylopoulos, J. and Levesque, H. (1983), 'An overview of knowledge representation'. In Brodie, Mylopoulos and Schmidt (1983). Reprinted in Ritchie and Albers (1983).

Nadathur, G. and Joshi, A.K. (1983), 'Mutual beliefs in conversational systems: Their role in referring expressions', Proceedings of IJCAI 1983, pp.603-605.

Nagao M. et al. (1982), 'An attempt to computerize dictionary data bases'. In Goetschalckx and Rolling (1982), pp.51-73.

Nagao, M. et al. (1985), 'The Japanese government project for machine translation', Computational Linguistics, vol. 11, pp. 91-110.

Nancarrow, P.H. (1981), 'A brief account of the development and first major installation of the Ideo-matic Chinese character encoder', ALLC Bulletin, vol.8, pp.263-265.

Newell, A. (1973), 'Production systems: models of control structure'. In Chase, W.G. (ed.), Visual Information Processing, New York, Academic Press, pp.463-526.

Newell, A. (1975), 'A tutorial on speech understanding systems'. In Reddy (1975).

Newmeyer, F. (1980), Linguistic Theory in America, New York, Academic Press.

Newmeyer, F. (1983), Grammatical Theory, Chicago, University of Chicago Press.

Norling-Christensen, O. (1982), 'Commercial lexicography on the threshold of the electronic age'. In Goetschalckx and Rolling (1982), pp.211-219.

O'Neill, H. (ed.) (1979), Procedures for Instructional Systems Development, New York, Academic Press.

O'Shea, T. and Eisenstadt, M. (eds) (1984), Artificial Intelligence: Tools, Techniques and Applications, New York, Harper and Row.

Oddy, R.N., Robertson, S.E., van Rijsbergen, C.J. and Williams, P.W. (eds) (1981), Information Retrieval Research, London, Butterworths.

Oettinger, A.G. (1963), 'The state of the art of automatic language translation: an appraisal'. In H. Marchl (ed.), Beiträge zur Sprachkunde und Informationsverarbeitung, Band 1, Heft 2, Munich, Oldenbourg Vlg., pp.17-32.

Olsson, A.H. (1982), 'Copyright problems and use of computers'. In Goetschalckx and Rolling (1982), pp.239-248.

Opitz, K. (1983), 'On dictionaries for special registers'. In Hartmann (1983a), pp.53-64.

Otten, M. and Pacak, M.G. (1971), 'Intermediate languages for automatic language processing'. In Tou, J.J. (ed.), Software Engineering, COINS III, vol. 2, New York, Academic Press, pp.105-118.

Paice, C.D. (1977), Information Retrieval and the Computer, London, Macdonald & Jane's.

Paice, C.D. (1981), 'The automatic generation of literature abstracts: an approach based on the identification of self-indicating phrases'. In Oddy et al. (1981).

Palmer, F. (1971), Grammar, Harmondsworth, Penguin.

Pankowicz, Z.L. (1967), Draft of a commentary on ALPAC Report, Part I, Rome Air Development Center, Griffiss Air Force Base, Rome NY, March 1967; cited in Josselson (1971, p.47).

Paré, M. (1974), The University of Montreal's Banque de Terminologie, Nice, International Federation of Translators.

Petrick, S. (1981), 'Field-testing the transformational question answering (TQA) system', Proceedings of the 19th Annual Meeting of the Association for Computational Linguistics, pp.35-36.

Piotrowski, R.G. and Georgiev, H. (1974), 'La traduction automatique en URSS', Revue Roumaine de Linguistique, vol. 19, pp.73-79.

Radford, A. (1981), Transformational Syntax, Cambridge, Cambridge University Press.

Rahmstorf, G. and Ferguson, M. (eds) (1978), Proceedings of a Workshop on Natural Language for Interaction with Data Bases, International Institute for Applied Systems Analysis.

Rayward-Smith, V. (1983), A First Course in Formal Language Theory, Oxford, Blackwell.

Reddy, D. Raj. (ed.) (1975), Speech Recognition, New York, Academic Press.

Reichling, A. (1976), 'La banque de terminologie de la Commission des Communautés Européennes Luxembourg'. In AFTERM (1976).

Reichling, A. (1978), 'EURODICAUTOM - Possibilités et limites d'un systeme automatisé d'aide a la traduction', Proceedings of Vth International Congress on Applied Linguistics, Montreal.

Reichling, A. (1982), 'Summary of round table discussion'. In Goetschalckx and Rolling (1982), pp.265-267.

Rich, E. (1983), Artificial Intelligence, New York, McGraw-Hill.

van Rijsbergen, C.J. (1979), Information Retrieval, London, Butterworths.

Ritchie, G. (1983), 'Semantics in parsing'. In King (1983), pp.199-217.

Ritchie, G. and H. Thompson (1984), 'Natural language processing'. In O'Shea and Eisenstadt (1984), pp.358-388.

Ritchie, G. and Albers, G. (eds) (1983), 'Tutorial on Artificial Intelligence', Proceedings of IJCAI 1983.

Rondeau, G. (1981), Introduction a la terminologie, Montreal, CEC.

Rondeau, G. (forthcoming), Introduction to Terminology.

Rubinoff, M. and Yovits, M.C. (eds) (1976), Advances in Computers, vol. 15, New York, Academic Press.

Rumelhart, D. (1975), 'Understanding and summarizing brief stories'. In Laberge and Samuels (1975).

Sager, J.C. (1979), 'The computer and multilingualism at the European Commission', Lebende Sprachen, vol. 24, pp.103-108.

Sager, J.C. et al. (1980), English Special Languages, Wiesbaden, Brandstetter.

Sager, J.C. and McNaught, J. (1981a), Feasibility Study of the Establishment of a Terminological Data Bank in the UK, British Library Research and Development Report no. 5642, Manchester, Centre for Computational Linguistics, UMIST, CCL/UMIST Report no. 81/8.

Sager, J.C. and McNaught, J. (1981b), Selective Survey of Existing Data Banks in Europe, British Library Research and Development Report no. 5643, Manchester, Centre for Computational Linguistics, UMIST, CCL/UMIST Report no. 81/9.

Sager, J.C. and McNaught, J. (1981c), Specifications of a Linguistic Data Bank for the UK, British Library Research and Development Report no. 5644, Manchester, Centre for Computational Linguistics, UMIST, CCL/UMIST Report no. 81/10.

Sager, J.C. and Price, L.E. (1983), The British Term Bank Project, Manchester, Centre for Computational Linguistics, UMIST, CCL/UMIST Report no. 83/14.

Salton, G. (1970), 'Automatic text analysis', Science, vol. 168, pp.335-343.

Salton, G. (ed.) (1971), The SMART Retrieval System: Experiments in Automatic Document Processing, Englewood Cliffs, N.J., Prentice Hall.

Salton, G. and McGill, M.J. (1983), Introduction to Modern Information Retrieval, New York, McGraw-Hill.

Schank, R. and Abelson, R. (1977), Scripts, Plans, Goals and Understanding, Hillsdale, N.J., Lawrence Erlbaum.

Schank, R.C., Kolodner, J.K. and DeJong, G. (1981), 'Conceptual information retrieval'. In Oddy et al. (1981).

Schulz, J. and Göricke, H. (1977), 'The dictionary in the computer: possibilities of directly interrogating a multilingual Terminology Data Bank via video display units', Babel, vol. 1.

Searle, J. (1969), Speech Acts, Cambridge, Cambridge University Press.

Sidner, C. (1979), 'Discourse and reference components of PAL'. In Metzing (1979).

Sidner, C.L. (1983), 'What the speaker means: the recognition of speaker's plans in discourse', International Journal of Computers and Mathematics, vol. 9.

Siklossy, L. (1977), Question-Asking Question-Answering, Report TR-71, Univ. of Texas Dept of Computer Sciences, Austin.

Siklossy, L. (1978), 'Impertinent question-answering systems: Justification and theory', Proceedings of ACM National Conference, pp.39-44.

Siliakus, H. (1984), 'To list, or not to list? Computer-aided word lists for the humanities and social sciences'. In Hartmann (1984), pp.420-424.

Simmons, R.F. (1970), 'Natural language question-answering systems: 1969', Communications of the ACM, vol. 13, pp.15-30.

Simmons, R.F. (1984), Computations from the English, Englewood Cliffs, N.J., Prentice-Hall.

Sleeman, D. and Brown, S.J. (eds) (in press), Intelligent Tutoring Systems, London, Academic Press.

Slocum, J. (1983), 'A status report on the LRC machine translation system', Proceedings of the Conference on Applied Natural Language Processing, pp.166-173. Association for Computational Linguistics.

Slocum, J. (1984), 'Machine translation: its history, current status, and future prospects'. In COLING (1984), pp.546-561.

Slocum, J. (1985a), 'METAL: The LRC machine translation system'. In King (1985b).

Slocum, J. (ed.) (1985b), Special issue of Computational Linguistics on machine translation.

Smirnitskij, I. and Akhmanova, O.S. (1948/77), Russko-Anglijskij Slovar'/Russian-English Dictionary, Moscow, G.I.S.

Smith, L.C. (1980), 'Implications of artificial intelligence for end user use of online systems', Online Review, vol. 4, pp.383-391.

Smith, N. (ed.) (1982), Mutual Knowledge, New York, Academic Press.

Smith, N. and D. Wilson (1979), Modern Linguistics, Harmondsworth, Penguin.

Snell, B.M. (ed.) (1979), Translating and the Computer, Amsterdam, North-Holland.

Snell, B. (ed.) (1983), Term Banks for Tomorrow's World, London, Aslib.

Snell-Hornby, M. (1984), 'The bilingual dictionary - help or hindrance'. In Hartmann (1984), pp.274-281.

Somers, H.L. (1983), 'The dynamic dictionary part of the sentence analyser PTOSYS'. In Holmboe, H. (ed.), Nordisk Forskerkursus om Datamatunderstøttet Leksikografi, Arhus, Institut for Lingvistik, Aarhus Universitet, pp.54-67.

Somers, H.L. and Johnson, R.L. (1979), 'PTOSYS, an interactive system for "understanding" texts using a dynamic strategy for creating and updating dictionary entries'. In MacCafferty, M. and Gray, K. (eds) The Analysis of Meaning, Informatics 5, London, Aslib, pp.85-103.

Somers, H. (1985), Valency and Case in Computational Linguistics, Edinburgh, Edinburgh University Press.

Sparck Jones, K. (1971), Automatic Keyword Classification for Information Retrieval, London, Butterworths.

Sparck Jones, K. (1974), Automatic Indexing 1974: A State of the Art Review, Univ. of Cambridge Computer Lab., Cambridge, UK.

Sparck Jones, K. and Kay, M. (1972), Linguistics and Information Science, New York, Academic Press.

Sparck Jones, K. and Wilks, Y. (eds.) (1983), Automatic Natural Language Parsing, Chichester, Ellis Horwood.

Stefik, M., Aikins, J., Balzer, R., Benoit, J., Birnbaum, L., Hayes-Roth, F. and Sacerdoti, E. (1982), The Organization of Expert Systems: A Prescriptive Tutorial, Report VLSI-82-1, Xerox, Palo Alto, California.

Sundström, E. (1978a), 'Introducing TNC and the TERMDOK System', International Classification, vol. 5, no. 2.

Sundström, E. (1978b), The TERMDOK System, fourth revised edition, Stockholm, TNC.

Sundström, E. (ed.) The Termdok Bulletin (nos. 1 - 46 published by TNC, Stockholm; nos. 47 onwards appear in International Classification, Saur, Munich).

TAUM (Traduction Automatique de l'Université de Montréal) (1973), 'Le système de traduction automatique de l'Université de Montréal (TAUM)', META, vol. 18, pp.227-289.

Tedd, L.A. (1979), Case studies in computer-based bibliographic information services, British Library R&D report no. 5463.

Tennant, H. (1981), Natural Language Processing, New York, Petrocelli.

Terminology and Documentation Directorate (1977), The Terminology Bank of Canada: an Overview, Ottawa, Term. and Doc. Dir.

Thouin, B. (1982), 'Le système METEO', Multilingua, vol. 1, pp.159–165.

TNC (ed.) (1980), TERMDOK in 3RIP – A Term Bank supported by an Interactive Text Data Base System, Stockholm, TNC.

Toma, P. (1976), 'An operational machine translation system'. In Brislin, R. W. (ed.), Translation: Applications and Research, New York, Gardner Press, pp.247–259.

Toma, P. (1977), 'Systran as a multilingual machine translation system'. In CEC (1977), vol. 1, pp.569–581.

Tomaszczcyk, J. (1983), 'The case for bilingual dictionaries for foreign language learners'. In Hartmann (1983a), pp.41–51.

Tomaszczcyk, J. (1984), 'The culture-bound element in bilingual dictionaries'. In Hartmann (1984), pp.289–297.

Tucker, A.B. (1984), 'A perspective on machine translation: theory and practice', Communications of the ACM, vol. 27, pp.322–329.

Tucker, A. and Nirenburg, S. (1984), 'Machine translation: a contemporary view', Annual Review of Information Science and Technology, vol. 19, pp.129–160.

Ullman, J.D. (1980), Principles of Data Base Systems, Potomac, Computer Science Press.

van Slype, G. (1979), 'Systran: evaluation of the 1978 version of the Systran English-French automatic system of the Commission of the European Communities', Incorporated Linguist, vol. 18, pp.86–89.

van Slype, G. (1982), 'Conception d'une methodologie generale d'evaluation de la traduction automatique', Multilingua, vol. 1, pp.221–237.

van Sterkenburg, P., Martin, W., and Al, B. (1982), 'A new Van Dale Project: Bilingual dictionaries on one and the same monolingual basis'. In Goetschalckx and Rolling (1982), pp.231–237.

Varile, G.B. (1983), 'Charts: a data structure for parsing'. In King (1983), pp.73–87.

Vauquois, B. (1975), La traduction automatique'a Grenoble, Paris, Dunod.

Vauquois, B. (1981), 'L'informatique au service de la traduction'. In Kittredge (1981a), pp.8–17.

Vauquois, B. and Boitet, C. (1985), 'Automated translation at Grenoble University', Computational Linguistics, vol. 11, pp. 28-36.

Vollmer, J. (1979) 'EURODICAUTOM: Bilan d'une experience', Proceedings of International Symposium on Theoretical and Methodological Problems of Terminology, Moscow.

Vollnhals, O. (1984), 'Utilization of a commercial linguistic database system for electronic storage and automated production of dictionaries'. In Hartmann (1984), pp.430-434.

Wahlster, W., Marburger, H., Jameson, A., Busemann, S. (1983), 'Over-answering yes-no questions: extended responses in a NL interface to a vision system', Proceedings of IJCAI 1983, pp.643-646.

Walker, D., Karlgren, H. and Kay, M. (1977), Natural Language in Information Science, FID publication, Stockholm, Skriptor AB.

Walker, D.E. (1981), 'The organization and use of information: contributions of information science, computational linguistics and artificial linguistics', Journal of the American Society of Information Science, pp.347-363.

Waltz, D.L. (ed.) (1977), 'Natural language interfaces'. ACM SIGART Newsletter, no. 61, pp.16-64.

Waltz, D.L. (1978), 'An English language question answering system for a large relational data base', Communications of the ACM, vol. 21, pp.526-539.

Weaver, W. (1949), 'Translation'. In Locke and Booth (1955), pp.15-23.

Webber, B.L. (1983), 'Pragmatics and database question answering', Proceedings of IJCAI 1983, pp.1204-1205.

Webber, B. and Joshi, A. (1982), 'Taking the initiative in natural language data base interactions'. In Horecky (1982), pp.413-418.

Webber, B.L. and Mays, E. (1983), 'Varieties of user misconceptions: detection and correction', Proceedings of IJCAI 1983, pp.650-652.

Webber, B., Joshi, A., Mays, E., and McKeown, K. (1983), 'Extended natural language database interaction', International Journal of Computers and Mathematics, vol. 9.

Wegner, P. (ed.) (1979), Research Directions in Software Technology, Cambridge, Mass., MIT Press.

Weischedel, R.M. and Black, J. (1980), 'Responding to potentially unparseable sentences', American Journal of Computational Linguistics, vol. 6, pp.97-109.

Wheeler, P.J. (1985), Article in King (1985b).

Whitelock, P.J., Johnson, R. and Bennett, P. (1984), The UMIST translation system, CCL/UMIST Report no. 84/3, Centre for Computational Linguistics, University of Manchester Institute of Science and Technology.

Wilensky, R. (1977), 'PAM: A program that infers intentions', Proceedings of IJCAI 1977.

Wilks, Y. (1973a), 'An Artificial Intelligence approach to machine translation'. In Schank, R.C. and Colby, K.M. (eds), Computer Models of Thought and Language, San Francisco, W.H. Freeman, pp.114-151.

Wilks, Y. (1973b), 'The Stanford machine translation project'. In Rustin, R. (ed.), Natural Language Processing, New York, Algorithmics Press, pp.243-290.

Wilss, W. (1982), The Science of Translation: Problems and Methods, Tübingen, Gunter Narr Verlag.

Winograd, T. (1975), 'Frame representations and the declarative-procedural controversy'. In Bobrow, D.G. and Collins, A. (eds), Representation and Understanding, New York, Academic Press, pp.185-210.

Winograd, T. (1983), Language as a Cognitive Process, vol. 1., Syntax, Reading, Mass., Addison-Wesley.

Winston, P. (1977), Artificial Intelligence, Reading, Mass., Addison-Wesley.

Woods, W.A. (1973), 'Progress in natural language understanding: an application to lunar geology', Proceedings of the National Computer Conference, Montvale, N.J., AFIPS Press, pp.441-450.

Woods, W.A., Kaplan, R.M. and Nash-Webber, B. (1972), The Lunar Sciences Natural Language Information System, Final Report, Report 2378, Bolt, Beranek and Newman, Cambridge, Mass.

Yngve, V.H. (1964), 'Implications of mechanical translation research', Proceedings of the American Philosophical Society, vol. 108, pp.275-281.

Yngve, V.H. (1967), 'MT at M.I.T. 1965'. In Booth, A.D. (ed.), Machine Translation, Amsterdam, North-Holland, pp.451-523.

Zave, P. (1984), 'The operational vs. the conventional approach to software design', Communications of the ACM, vol. 27, pp.104-118.

Zgusta, L. (1971), Manual of Lexicography, The Hague, Mouton.

Zgusta, L. (1984), 'Translational equivalence in the bilingual dictionary'. In Hartmann (1984), pp.147-154.

Zorkoczy, P. (1982), Information Technology, London, Pitman.